Two On the Aisle

A JUDAIC AMERICAN TALE OF ROMANCE AND CREATIVE DREAMS

David A. Horowitz

Dedicated to the memory of

Nathan Horowitz
(1908–1994)

and

Dorothy Levine Horowitz
(1917–1990)

June 7, 2019

David:
Let's keep the
creative juices flowing!
David A. Horowitz

It is the heart of man I am trying to imply ...

WILLIAM SAROYAN

TABLE OF CONTENTS

PREFACE i

CHAPTER 1 Nathan's Baggage 4
The Old Country | Migrations | Street Urchin | A Place in the Sun |
Wages | The Poet | The Catskills | The Crash | Redemption

CHAPTER 2 Dorothy's Dreams 22
Broadway Casino | The Levines | A World to Win | Rescue | Star-Crossed |
The Lure of Celluloid | Dialectics | An Unlikely Union

CHAPTER 3 Bronx Tales 42
Tender Comrades | The Good Things | A Million Laughs | Family
Planning | Davidovitch | VJ Kid | Back in the Bronx | Imperfect

CHAPTER 4 Moving On Up 62
Living for the City | Culture | Getting On | Greener Pastures | Faith |
Hollywood Boulevard | Tin Waltz | July 24, 1954 | Bess | Exodus

CHAPTER 5 This Side of Paradise 86
Refuge | Corona | Westwinds | At Home with the Muse | September 13,
1958 | Choices | Mrs. Goodfriend | Generations | Hair | 1968 | Schisms

CHAPTER 6 The Perils of Success 109
Firing Line | A Far Cry | The Most of Life | The Quiet Man | Undone |
Great Expectations | Worldly Vistas | Separate Ways | Gone West

CHAPTER 7 Golden Rays 129
The Pier | A Yiddish Heart | Our Young and Old | My *Feh* Lady |
Twilight Village | Family Ties | Warriors

CHAPTER 8 Sunlight and Shadows 146
Not Yet | Peace Talk | Figarow | Here! | Believing | Roots | Bread and
Butter Lines | The Pact

CHAPTER 9 Fate 162
Hegira | The New and the Old | Once Too Often | Life and Loss | What
There Was | Job Revisited

CHAPTER 10 Legacies 176
What Else | Give Pause | Tribute | Candlelight

CHAPTER 11 Echoes 187
Two on the Aisle | Markers | Reverberations | Carrying On

APPENDIX 198

Chronological List of Published Works 202

PREFACE

Sometime in the mid-1980s, Nathan and Dorothy Horowitz met with the president of their California synagogue to reserve a cemetery plot. Not long after, Nathan took to poetry to describe the encounter. After years of patient relegation to the balcony and the sidelines, he exclaimed, he finally had secured "two on the aisle!"

Two on the Aisle: A Judaic American Tale of Romance and Creative Dreams recounts the odyssey of two seemingly ordinary Americans whose desire for a materially rewarding, ethically balanced, and creative life offers a distinctive story.

The saga begins with the historic migration of immigrant parents from Eastern Europe and an account of childhood and early adulthood in the Jewish quarters of early twentieth century New York. From there the story moves on to the devastating impact of the Great Depression of the 1930s, an unlikely marriage, and the struggle to build a family amid the dislocations of World War II. As Nathan becomes a sales representative for a chemical products company, the narrative proceeds to an account of lower-middle-class life in the postwar Bronx and the plebeian resorts of the Catskill Mountains. It then chronicles a move to the Long Island suburbs, Dorothy's belated career as a teacher and guidance counselor in the New York City public school system, and the couple's relocation to a gated community in southern California.

At first glance, the story of Nathan and Dorothy Horowitz typifies the path to economic security and professional standing taken by many working-class offspring of Jewish immigrants in the post-Depression years. Yet their tale has two distinguishing features.

First, Dorothy's secular socialist roots and Nathan's Orthodox upbringing require constant negotiation over these polarities of Jewish American culture. After years of grappling with their own religious, cultural, and political identity, both find they must react to their sons' immersion in the social and cultural ferment of the 1960s and '70s, to the problematic prospects of Jewish grandchildren, and to the next generation's lukewarm relationship to the State of Israel.

The second distinctive theme of the narrative relates to the literary and theatrical ambitions Nathan and Dorothy cherish from adolescence.

Most of Dorothy's early poetry, short stories, dramatizations, and skits reflect the socialist political convictions of her youth. Yet her professional career as an educator and subsequent service in a Jewish women's organization in California provide new venues for her talents. At the same time, she continues to produce a variety of highly personal poems, short stories, and dramatic pieces, both published and unpublished, that present disarming perspectives on marriage, gender, social mores, suburbia, retirement, old age, and mortality.

Nathan's youthful production of literary works includes Yiddish dialect pieces, lyrics for Negro spirituals, assorted short stories and sketches, and reams of poetry. He never achieves the Depression-born dream of becoming a Hollywood screenwriter. Yet he and Dorothy author a three-act play that enjoys a brief run in an off-Broadway venue in the mid-1950s while he continues to produce Yiddish flavored verse, parodies, and dramatic farces. Once retired, he expands his production of poetry, completes an unpublished memoir, and has several pieces appear in the English language edition of the Yiddish *Forward*. As Nathan's efforts gain a token of regional and national recognition during his residence at a senior facility in Portland, Oregon in the early 1990s, he records personal impressions in a daily journal that joins light hearted banter with stark prose addressing existential themes of aging, loss, and death.

Two on the Aisle incorporates excerpts from the extensive collections of both writers to reveal how the liberating forces of principled intellect, creativity, and humor can serve to humanize the challenges, struggles, and minor triumphs ordinary people experience. The couple's willingness to provide a disarmingly honest testament of their hopes, fantasies, inner thoughts, and disappointments offers a legacy of perseverance by two eloquent yet relatively unheralded observers and dramatists of the human condition.

From the perspective of a professional historian like myself, the tale of Nathan and Dorothy Horowitz offers a window into the complexities and contradictions of the modern Jewish American experience. Yet the challenge of telling their story assumes an added dimension because Nathan and Dorothy were my parents. *Two on the Aisle* is, by necessity, a hybrid work. In part, it offers an exploration of cultural history based on documentary evidence drawing upon surviving letters and a library of published and unpublished creative work. Yet the narrative also serves as a family memoir and personal reminiscence in which the author appears as a secondary but significant character. In both cases, however, the time-honored requirement of reconstructing the past in as truthful and compassionate manner as possible remains the same.

David A. Horowitz
Portland and Arch Cape, Oregon

1

NATHAN'S BAGGAGE

At the end of 1937, as a second wave of the Great Depression took hold, Nathan Horowitz raised two thousand dollars to buy the coat room concession at Gottlieb's, a midtown Manhattan restaurant. He and Dorothy Levine planned to marry that February, a month after the prospective bride's graduation from New York City's Hunter College. Purchased at Bloomingdale's Department Store, her white gold wedding band cost $6.98. The printed invitations, issued in the name of both sets of parents, announced the event for February 23rd, the day after George Washington's Birthday, since the restaurant had booked a large party for the holiday that promised good tips at the cloak room.

The Old Country

Nathan came from humble origins. His father, who went by the name Barnett Ariovich, and his mother, Becky Gollop (Golub), were Eastern European Jewish immigrants from Radun, a Belorussian (now Belarus) village of some thousand people thirty miles south of Vilna, the historic capital of Lithuania. A large Jewish population had resided in the area, known as "Russian Poland," for five hundred years. Since czarist edicts restricted land ownership and choice of occupations to Gentiles, however, the Jews served mainly as artisans and retail proprietors. The bustling *shtetl* boasted a wide array of small shops and Jewish institutions, including the prestigious Yeshiva (theological seminary), founded in 1869 by the famed Rabbi Israel Meir Kahan, subsequently bestowed the title, *Chofetz Haim* ("one who wants life").

Barnett, whose given name was Berel, was born in 1881, the year a series of devastating pogroms victimized Jewish communities following the assassination of Czar Alexander II. Barnett's father was Hillel Ariovich, a shoemaker renowned for surviving four wives before he died well into his nineties. Five brothers worked the family trade. Becky (the shortened version of Rebecca, a variation on Rifka) was one of eight children. She was born three days after her future husband to Avrom Duvid (Abraham David) and Geneshe Golub in a house three door down from Barnett's family. Avrom had attended the Yeshiva but made a living as a dairy farmer and brick maker. Becky would recall how she and her brothers and sisters carried bricks to the kiln and sang throughout the nights while tending the fires:

"*Oi,* How's New York?—What is America?—How do they eat in America?—How do they live in America?—Do they have chairs in America?"

After a stint as a servant in the homes of Vilna's affluent Jewish families, Becky returned to Radun at age seventeen to bake goods for Russian soldiers at the tea house her mother now ran. It was a lively place, she remembered. Occasionally she sang and danced for the patrons to the accompaniment of a revered older brother, a musician and sign painter who had made his own violin. Barnett would later entertain his children with stories of untethered goats, unhinged gates, and young people romping across the village fields. Yet the twentieth century brought an intensification of Jewish persecution. Just past the age of twenty, Barnett feared conscription in the czar's army under a Russian law requiring Jewish families to pay 150 rubles to exempt sons from military service. Young Ariovich and Rifka Golub soon announced their engagement. Barnett immediately set forth for London, where he soon wrote for her to come.

Becky Golub vividly recalled the day in 1901 when she said good-bye. Her father "started kissing me—he couldn't talk," she remembered. Four children left in one year, part of a historic migration that would empty Eastern Europe of one third of its Jewish population. Becky traveled with a group of seven or eight young women to Lubava (Libau), a Latvian port on the Baltic Sea then part of East Prussia, and then paid the equivalent of thirty-five dollars for a three-day Danish steamer and train journey to London. Their destination was Stepney, the island's most populated locality, the predominantly Jewish district of Whitechapel in the city's East End, where the girls made their way to a Jewish charity shelter for temporary housing.

Uneasy about the huge influx of rural Eastern Europeans, England's Jewish religious leaders encouraged proper weddings among Stepney's newcomers, three-quarters of whom were under the age of thirty-five. In December 1901, Barnett and Becky married at the United Synagogue on Duke's Place, the center of Orthodox Jewish life in London. Becky remembered with some bitterness that the rabbi administered simultaneous wedding rites to a number of couples and that wealthy and poor congregants sat in separate sections of the sanctuary. Nevertheless, she proudly displayed the framed wedding license on the wall of the couple's flat so no one could accuse them of a socialist-style "free marriage."

Migrations

Living on Commercial Road near the Charles Street Market, the couple struggled to survive in a strange environment. Barnett had difficulty finding work but finally hired on as a low-wage assistant to a clothing factory presser. Unfamiliar with the trade, he burned his face during the first week on the job while testing the heat of the eighteen-pound gas iron, the first appearance of a malady that would last his forty-year lifetime "in shop." Like many Jewish wives, Becky stayed at home to run the household and manage family finances. On an errand one day, she confronted a horrendous fog that burned her eyes so badly she could barely see. Hopelessly lost in an unfamiliar city where she barely spoke the language, she began to cry until a man in a high hat took her by the hand to the bus stop at the corner, paid her fare to Commercial Road, and told the driver to make sure that she got off at the right stop.

Samuel, Becky and Barnett's first child, was born in January 1903, most likely at nearby London Hospital, where Jewish charity groups provided kosher food. It was at the hospital, Becky later claimed, that the "*missionairen*" (missionaries) assigned the family the more common name of Horowitz. Although her children would assume the culprit was the Salvation Army, the name change probably originated with London's Jewish Board of Guardians, the major immigrant aid organization for Eastern Europeans. Whitechapel was the corridor for Russian Jews seeking access to the Americas. Anxious about Great Britain's ability to absorb large numbers of impoverished migrants and risk an anti-Semitic backlash, Jewish agencies encouraged newcomers to relocate and worked with the Jewish Colonization Society to subsidize Atlantic passenger ship travel.

Once a cousin in Boston encouraged Becky to migrate, assuring her there was no fog in America, she "went to the people who give tickets to the boat," as she later explained, and secured free booking in steerage. The cold, fourteen-day winter's voyage to Halifax, Nova Scotia left Barnett, but not Becky, violently seasick. After traveling by rail to the U.S. border and passing a cursory medical exam, they boarded a second train for Boston. Becky remembered trudging through the snow to a friend's house in Dorchester with a newborn infant in her arms and no boots or a proper overcoat. After a brief stay, Barnett left for New York City, where he secured a job in his trade as a garment presser. The family soon reunited in a two-room tenement on Hester Street on the Lower East Side of Manhattan where amenities included a cold-water sink in the hall and a backyard outhouse.

Street Urchin

Ever on the lookout to improve the lot of her brood, Becky found new quarters on Monroe Street, followed by a flat next to a stable on Cherry

Street, down the block from where Israel Baline, the future songwriter Irving Berlin, lived with his Russian family. To make ends meet, Becky took in four boarders, for whom she cooked, washed, and made beds. To add to the travails of immigrant life, the couple lost their second child at age two to diphtheria. Then, on a hot Friday night on September 11, 1908, Barnett retreated to the barbershop while a midwife delivered Nathan, soon to be known as Nady or *Nutilla*, on the kitchen table. Two years later, the family welcomed a daughter, Augusta (Gussie).

As a presser for a series of establishments in the West Seventh Avenue garment district below 42nd Street, Barnett spent ten to twelve hours a day at the shop. An avid reader of Yiddish socialist newspapers such as the *Jewish Day* and *The Forward* and a loyal member of the Amalgamated Clothing Workers, he had little use for workplace brass:

"The bosses should boin" (burn), he liked to say in fractured English.

Barnett's class-conscious outbursts belied his normal good humor and taste for the finer things. A studio photograph of the period shows the mustached and confident family head in a bowler hat, fine leather shoes and gloves, and an expensive topcoat with a velvet collar and trim. Entwining her husband's arm, Becky stares directly at the camera across her high cheekbones, proudly sporting a feathered headdress, well-fitting gloves, a black leather handbag, and a lambskin coat with fur collar. Sometime after posing for the picture, she leased a candy store in East Harlem, allowing her to apply entrepreneurial skills learned from her Radun family. The extra income permitted a move from the Lower East Side to a four-room, third-floor "walk-up" apartment on East 100th Street that boasted hot water and an inside toilet.

At five or six years of age, curly-haired Nady took to the streets. He mastered the technique of hitching rides on the trolley cars moving back and forth from the nearby Lexington Avenue Barns. Short of stature, he responded to taunts from older boys by learning to duck under thrown objects and becoming the fastest runner on the block. Soon he and sister Gussie assumed the task of meeting their father at the Third Avenue Elevated station at the close of work. Barnett would give them a nickel to go to the back entrance of the local saloon to fill a tin pail with beer for the trip home, taking care not to spill a drop.

Sometime in 1914, Becky arranged for relocation to the East Bronx, a next rung of mobility for denizens of the Lower East Side. Nady now attended Public School 53, an imposing structure sitting above six flights of granite steps, over which his mother escorted him daily. Yet Yiddish, not English, was his first language, the school was not his home, and he longed for the freedom of the streets. Besides, his teachers forced the natural "lefty" to scrawl with his right hand. Learning to sit with hands folded on the desk and required to respond with "yes, ma'am," the wily street urchin dutifully combed his hair, sang the Star Spangled Banner, and recited an early form of the Pledge of Allegiance, then in its twenty-second year.

Nady much preferred Sundays in nearby Crotona Park, where he and his father munched Indian nuts and the boy occasionally sold lollipops. A photograph from the park shows the young lad wearing homemade knickers, his arms around both parents, his face somewhere between an ingratiating smile and a comfortable smirk. Another picture has him fingering the strings of a Pancho Villa sombrero half-cocked on his head. At home, Barnett insisted upon introducing the family to high culture. Before any of his neighbors, he bought a hand-cranked Victrola to play 78 rpm. Red Seal recordings of opera star Enrico Caruso and Jewish violinists Mischa Elman and Jascha Heifetz. Barnett even bought a piano for children's music lessons and arranged to have Nady learn the violin until the teacher advised the family to save its money.

On the move once again, Becky secured a four-room, third-floor "walk-up" facing the street. Although quarter meters still governed the gas lighting, the tenement featured a dumbwaiter allowing tenants to dispatch garbage to the janitor in the basement. In this close East Bronx community, neighbors socialized when they could in Claremont Park and often returned to the Horowitz flat for a glass of hot tea. Meanwhile, Nady continued to struggle at his new school. Divided into morning and afternoon sessions, the ancient, overcrowded P.S. 42 featured outdoor toilets that emptied into open trenches. When asked what he wanted to be when he grew up, Nady passed by the usual firefighter, police officer, or soldier. Instead, he said he would like to be an actor, a confession that reflected his fascination with theatrics but precipitated the howling mirth of the entire class, including the teacher.

Summers at Uncle Solomon Golub's dairy farm in North Middleboro, Massachusetts provided respite from the simmering city pavements until Solomon convinced Barnett to go into the junk business. To Becky's dismay, the experiment lasted only a week when her husband proved incapable of soliciting strangers for merchandise. The next move was to Boston's West Side, where Becky's mother, Geneshe, and her two youngest daughters, Sadie and Eva, had settled after immigrating from

Radun. Eva, the most Americanized of the sisters, involved herself in flute lessons, socialism, the labor movement, and woman suffrage. Becky was more interested in freeing Barnett from the deterioration of his legs induced by stand-up labor. Accordingly, she bought a downtown kosher restaurant in 1917 for $475.

The La Grange Street eatery proved a spectacular success. Becky and five waiters provided 150 people a night with forty-five cent dinners that included soup, meat, chicken, *kishke* (stuffed beef sausage), bread, and pudding. As with many immigrant enterprises, everyone slept in the upstairs rooms while the restaurant served as dining and living quarters. For Nady, the location required an eight-block walk to a school in which there were only three or four other Jewish boys. Bullied by Irish and Italian Catholic rivals, he learned to fight for his life and then run, although the trauma of these confrontations left him with an abiding distrust of Gentiles and sensitivity to any hint of anti-Semitism.

Never backing down from a challenge, the pint-sized nine-year-old insisted on supplementing family income by peddling newspapers in the Boston subways. The stale underground air, however, proved his undoing when he contracted a virulent form of the global influenza pandemic coinciding with the final stages of the Great War (World War I). After four days in a comatose state, Nady stirred to consciousness as a visiting physician solemnly took his pulse and his parents hovered over him. Once the crisis passed, however, Becky had to contend with Barnett, who missed the Bronx neighborhood and the camaraderie of workers at the shop.

In contrast to his wife, the Horowitz patriarch remained unable to adjust to the rituals of commerce or the servility of running a restaurant. After horrendous late-night arguments, an exasperated Becky saw no choice but to give up her dream of running a family business. Despite the fact that she had turned the eatery into a virtual gold mine, she sold the restaurant back to the previous owners. Not surprisingly, this turn of events merely reinforced Barnett's sense of uselessness. The result was a severe bout of depression, diagnosed by a visiting physician as "the blues." When hefty doses of Bromo-Seltzer induced an apparent recovery, the grateful patient returned to the garment shop and the family reunited in New York.

"Another slam of the iron," Barnett liked to say in Yiddish.

A Place in the Sun

By the early 1920s, a presser's wages were sufficient to facilitate a move to a four-room, coal stove-heated unit in the rear of an East Bronx tenement along the Third Avenue "El." Spared the clatter of the overhead trains, the flat nevertheless opened to dark courtyards and dingy air shafts, leaving Nady with a lifetime fixation on adequate light. As in most of the period's apartment buildings, the hallways smelled of cooking and garbage. Yet the teeming streets provided a fitting escape. During winters, Nady and his pals slid down the frozen slopes of Crotona Park on overturned milk can lids. Spring and summer found them shagging fly balls for the young Hank ("Bruggy") Greenberg, who would go on to become the greatest Jewish baseball slugger of all time as a first baseman for the Detroit Tigers. On other occasions, the boys contented themselves with sidewalk games such as "Johnny-on-the-Pony."

City life offered both opportunities and perils. Nady and his peers could earn tip money by informing nearby residents of incoming phone calls at the local drugstore. When a friend built a homemade crystal radio set, Nady listened in wonder as fiddle music miraculously penetrated the airwaves. At the same time, survival on the streets depended upon negotiating the good graces of neighborhood hoodlums like "Bricksie," "Skunk," and "Benny the Ape" who commanded the underside of tenement stairways or remote rooftops for lucrative crap games. As Nady later recalled, the first of the trio went on to the electric chair, the second "disappeared," and the third ultimately graduated to radical politics.

After-school hours required long stints at *Cheder* (Hebrew School), where mentors with tobacco-stained beards, nicotine-yellowed teeth, and onion-flavored breath taught their charges to read Torah, chant the proper prayers, and familiarize themselves with the historical sufferings of the Chosen People. Nady was deeply impressed with these lessons and became the most religiously observant member of the family, even wearing the Orthodox *talis* (fringed prayer vest) under his outer garments. He also observed strict Jewish dietary laws by never mixing meat and milk and avoiding shellfish and pork, a practice he never abandoned.

Although Barnett was a casual Jew, religion played a huge role in family ritual. A highlight was Becky's Friday evening meals inaugurating the Sabbath. Homemade specialties included roast chicken, freshly baked loaves of *chaleh* bread, potato *kugel*, and noodles, not to mention *gefilte* fish spiked with horseradish, pickled herring mixed with green onions, chopped liver, nut-studded *lekach* desserts, and rows of irresistible rugelech pastries.

As Nady approached the age of thirteen in 1921, a tutor began to prepare him for the Hebrew recitation of his *Bar-Mitzvah* portion of the *Torah*. The initiation of Jewish manhood demanded a new fifteen-dollar double-breasted jacket with matching knickers and cap as well as a fresh pair of high-topped shoes. The rite of passage found its way into a studio photograph in which Nathan Horowitz proudly stands in his new outfit, the customary *talis* around his neck, his right hand leaning on a prayer book resting on a parlor table. Once the ceremony concluded at the *shul* (synagogue), family and friends arrived to enjoy Becky's *lotke* potato pancakes and cheese blintzes at the Third Avenue flat cleared of furniture and filled with chairs borrowed from the building's Italian, Hungarian, and Irish neighbors.

Bar-Mitzvah gifts included a variety of handkerchiefs and neckties, an inexplicable cut-glass fruit bowl, and two gold pieces worth two and five dollars. Days later, Sam took his brother to a stationery store and told him to pick out two books. Nady's first selection was *The Putnam Hall Boys*, a chronicle of the football adventures of a team of blue-eyed, blond military school students. The second was *The Works of William Shakespeare*. Sam's generosity was something of a mystery since he rarely had steady work after finishing eighth grade. Seeking to placate Barnett, who insisted that his oldest son learn a trade or be self-supporting, Becky would burst into the bedroom to rouse the recalcitrant job seeker to take to the streets. When he found a position, Sam would regale the supper table with insights into the complex organization he soon would be managing, only to abandon or lose the slot within a week or two.

Sam's inability to remain employed would leave Nathan with a lingering obsession over succeeding in the workplace. Meanwhile, the older son's unpredictability fed parental anxiety. Shortly after Nady's *Bar-Mitzvah*, Sam showed up at the door with a uniformed stranger.

"Who is this?" Becky stammered in Yiddish, her hand involuntarily raised to her throat in near panic.

Sam had joined the Marines.

Through much of the nineteenth century, Russian law made it difficult for Jewish boys to avoid military conscription. When enforced, these obligations virtually meant the abandonment of Jewish faith and identity, prompting many bereaved parents to enter the seven-day period of religious mourning when losing their sons this way. Barnett had fled conscription into the dreaded czar's army as a young man. A working-class socialist, he had come to view war as an imperialist tool of the hated bosses. Humiliated and hurt by his eldest son's betrayal, he vowed that Sam would never set foot in the house again.

Becky merely wrung her hands in a fit of helplessness.

Wages

Sam spent three years at South Carolina's Parris Island. To avoid anti-Semitic taunts, he changed his last name to Harris, a designation that subsequently would take on enormous significance for his younger brother. Becky eventually prevailed upon her husband to rescind the ban on their elder son's banishment. Yet visits for the Jewish holidays became points of contention when Sam sought to make extra cash by filling in for the observant help at the Tremont Avenue retail stalls.

While his brother sought to assimilate through the Marines, Nady fantasized about an American identity, which he attempted to fashion through creative writing. The brush with influenza had inspired his first poem, "A Mother's Prayer," a morbid portrait of parental grief for a lost soldier culminating with a fitting final couplet:

> And with a last look at the picture on the shelf,
> Through the window she flung herself.

However plodding these efforts appeared to be, Nathan's imaginative skills enabled him to excel in school at composing essays, creating rhymed verse, and reciting speeches.

An eighth grade poem, "I'm a Slafe," employed colloquial dialect to tell the story of a beleaguered working-class housewife whose husband verbally abuses her after she spends the day washing dishes, cleaning, wiping, and baking.

"Ef I can stand it," she cries out, "I'm made from iron!" a favorite phrase of Becky's.

Nathan's literary and dramatic talents were sufficient to overcome an inability to master mathematics and guarantee his selection to the Rapid Advance (R.A.). In its first year of operation, this experimental program of the New York public schools compressed three years of junior high into two. Once completing eighth grade in June 1922, three months before he turned fourteen, Nady graduated from P.S. 55. His autograph book contained a Yiddish inscription from his father, a wish for success from sister Gussie, and a selection of trite verses from schoolmates.

Becky was not present at the graduation. Still attempting to extricate her husband from the shop, she had purchased a boarding house in Tannersville, New York in the Catskill Mountains resort where one of Barnett's brothers was the *schochet*—the ritual kosher meat slaughterer. The summer business was the family's first experience with the Catskills. Situated one-hundred miles northwest of New York City, the area would attract nearly one million Jewish vacationers over the next fifty years. Eager to spare their wives and children the sweltering heat of New York summers, working-class breadwinners traveled by train, bus, hired "hacks," and later, cars, to join their families for weekend stays at modest boarding houses, bungalow colonies, and hotels not "restricted" to Gentiles. The communally oriented colonies and lush countryside reminded older visitors of the Old Country.

Barnett named the Tannersville boarding facility "Park View House" because the surrounding green hills, trees, and birds brought back memories of Radun. Yet the idyllic dream ended there. Despite (or because of) his congenial manner, Barnett proved to be a poor solicitor of patrons for the summer enterprise. Once again, Becky had to acknowledge that her husband did not have the temperament for the world of business. Returning to New York that fall, she opened a secret bank account out of fear that her beloved Barnett was not equipped for any other trade but garment pressing and that his ailing legs would not last forever.

Imagining himself as a source of financial assistance for the struggling family, Nady enrolled in the accounting program at Manhattan's High School of Commerce. Yet the freshman's poor math skills made this a disastrous choice. Failing to last the school year, he induced Barnett to sign his working papers. The fourteen-year-old dropout now inaugurated a fifty-one year odyssey in the world of labor.

Nady's first job was as a delivery boy for a dental lab. His second, as a metalworker in a dank Lower East Side factory, ended abruptly after the first day on his mother's orders when he came home with blood-blistered palms and bent fingers. When Becky learned that the bosses refused to pay the first day's wages, she put on her holiday dress and flowered hat, grabbed her five-foot son by the hand, took the subway downtown, and stormed into the establishment. As she read the riot act to the stunned management, awe-struck workers stopped their machinery in its tracks and watched in rapt attention as she compelled the employers to turn over the dollar and change they owed her progeny.

A four-dollars-a-day job as a plumber's assistant provided Nady's next opportunity. One assignment required him to carry six-foot lengths of four-inch cast-iron pipe across narrow beams strung fifteen stories above the ground, a traumatic experience given his fear of heights. He subsequently found work as a butcher's delivery boy and chicken plucker, an errand runner for a thread manufacturer, and a stockroom assistant for a textile firm.

Turning over his pay to his mother, Nady received a two-dollar-a-week allowance for carfare and expenses. Occasionally, Becky treated him to a premium forty-cent seat for the Saturday matinee at a first-run movie palace. More often, he thrilled to the exploits of silent film stars such as Tom Mix, William S. Hart, and William Farnum at the local theater, an experience no less diminished by the open door of the facility's toilet and the requirement that the ushers patrol the aisles with deodorant dispensers simultaneously designed to kill the cockroaches.

Out of work one afternoon in April 1923, the fifteen-year-old Nady walked down to Yankee Stadium to watch the gathering crowd for Opening Day of the new ballpark. Desperate to gain entry, he fell behind a Press Gate pass holder, silently imploring the man to vouch for him as they approached the guard. After selling his right-field seat for a dollar to a standing-room patron, Nady saw Governor Al Smith throw out the first pitch and witnessed the great Babe Ruth hit the park's first home run.

He walked all the way back to the East Bronx to avoid breaking the precious dollar bill.

The Poet

The following year, Becky successfully scouted a breezy four-room apartment in a four-story building with a court entrance, clean halls, and white porcelain kitchen sinks instead of cast-iron fixtures. Brother Sam now returned from the Marines with his new last name. Sister Gussie also fashioned an Americanized moniker. Having won a beauty contest at Theodore Roosevelt High School, she now answered to"Teddy." In 1926, the new apartment would be the site of her "Sweet Sixteen," for which her mother served ice cream and soda while maintaining a sharp eye on the kissing games.

Despite fractured English and a lack of schooling, Becky was thriving. She served as a charter member of the First Ladies Day Nursery of the Bronx, a charitable infant welfare center, and as president of the Radun Ladies Society of New York, the women's auxiliary of the village mutual-aid committee. To raise funds for the *Talmud Torah* (Jewish religious school) and other needs in the Old Country, she arranged with a photographer from a town near Radun to take pictures of the Jewish community's homes, shops, places of worship, social institutions, and streets. Then she placed Yiddish inscriptions beneath the images to identify the names of families and familiar sites, and had them converted to glass-lantern slides for public showings.

Becky's hand in the project is borne out by a photo of Radun's cantor posing before the graves of her father and Hillel Ariovich, Barnett's father. The fundraiser called for the Society to sell prints of the slides to "*lontzmen*" (countrymen) in New York. As secretary of the Massachusetts Friends of Radun Society, Becky's sister, Eva, now married to New Bedford dairy farmer and merchant Nathan Herman, received a similar set of glass slides.

While Becky prospered, Nady became his own worst nightmare. For a time he worked as a janitorial maintenance worker at four dollars a day moving dormitory furniture at Columbia University. He later sold shoes for a department store near the Empire State Building and then for a bargain basement outlet on 14th Street, the Mecca of working-class retail. Yet jobs were becoming harder to find by the late-1920s. He often spent lonely sessions in Central Park with his elbows hooked behind a park bench, fantasizing an escape from his father's failing legs and his own inadequacies. Sports offered one outlet. Nady played tin-can soccer, football, handball, and joined the Tremont Stars Athletic and Social Club basketball squad. His punch ball team, the Bronx Trumbenix (from *trumbenick*, Barnett's Yiddish nickname for his slow-growing son), won a citywide competition one year.

Nady's greatest passion continued to be creative writing. From the time he served as a plumber's assistant, he composed poems and stories during lunch breaks and evenings. While working in a textile company stockroom, he polished off "The Poet," a semi-autobiographical verse in dialect that captured the literary aspirations of a butcher boy:

A poiet, a poiet, I want to be,
I'll write from de montins, I'll write from de sea.

Later in the decade, he composed a dialect narrative called "Marvin"—a drama of the Bronx streets. A notebook of the period contains a self-effacing confession on the inside cover:

For years I've been searching in earnest endeavor
To write or do something real clever
But elusive this success, and wraith like all glory,
So still I'm a-chasing, and that's my damned story.

The Catskills

Fate appeared to have changed in 1927 when Nady survived a long line of applicants to become a stock clerk in the chintz and cretonne section of Macy's Department Store. He now wore a uniform—a gray jumper fashioned with the retailer's insignia. When Nady successfully auditioned for a two-line part in the store's annual Red Star Revue at the Brooklyn Academy of Music, he met an animated youngster of fifteen, a fellow employee from main floor silverware whose thin frame, shock of reddish-blond hair, and habitual grin caught his attention.

High school dropout Gershon (Gar) Kanin and Nady became fast friends, meeting as they raced down the "up" escalator and shared frantic lunches at vegetarian restaurants. Brought home to Gar's family, Nady discovered a new world of Jewish atheism, Marxian socialism, modernist aesthetics, and avant-garde theater. Gar's older brother Mike was an artist who painted burlesque flats. Mike Kanin also played guitar in the Red Peppers, a hot jazz combo featuring Gar on sax and a Kanin family friend, Charles Kingsford (Cohen), a composer and Juilliard music school graduate, on piano. Rising actors such as Sam Levene were regular house guests at the apartment. Nady discovered that the Brotherhood of Man, a concept he associated with the Torah, was now a universal banner of social justice.

Macy's management failed to offer steady work to either employee. Two years later, however, Gar talked his way into a position as a Catskills summer "social director" at a hotel in South Fallsburg. Supplied with samples of Nady's Yiddish dialect poems and stories, Gar found his friend a similar post at Gibber's Hemlocks in Kiamesha Lake. The Catskill resorts were to become the breeding ground of comedians such as Sid Caesar, Red Buttons, Buddy Hackett, Jerry Lewis, and Danny Kaye. Meanwhile, twenty-one-year-old Nady Horowitz was a suitable candidate for the resort trade. He had matured from an impish Bronx youngster into a streetwise sharpie whose near-six-foot athletic frame and jet-black curls created a stunning impression. A Bronx photo of the period shows him casually leaning against a stone block wall, left hand in the trouser pocket of a three-piece suit, a slouch hat jauntily tilted at the rear of his head.

Responsible for the hotel's entertainment, the new social director discovered a receptive audience for his Yiddish material, although his main task was to dance with the "midweek widows" awaiting Friday evening commutes from their New York husbands. At the close of the season, a striking blonde patron slipped the good-looking Bronx native a home phone number with a note asking him to call any Wednesday night.

He never did. Wednesday was basketball evening at the gym.

The Crash

As it turned out, the end of the summer preceded the October 1929 stock market crash by a matter of weeks. As economic activity dropped by half and unemployment skyrocketed to a disastrous 25 percent over the next few years, the aspirations of an entire generation of Americans evaporated in smoke. Nady Horowitz's salvation was a position as a solicitor for the Kaplan Clinic, a shady medical facility managed by two West Indians known as the Derrick Brothers. He was to scout the undergarment factories below 34th Street for prospective clients who had suffered injuries at work and were entitled by a recent New York State workers' compensation statute to free medical care covered by employer insurance.

Since solicitors received bounties for each client, a fierce competition emerged among the "bloodhounds" of rival clinics. One outfit might accrue referrals by distributing handbills, erecting posters, or bribing employers with free tin medicine cabinets filled with the cheapest first-aid supplies required by law. Yet competitors frequently tore down posters and cabinets and even scraped rival names off donated antiseptic containers. The only way to prevail was with in-house spies, normally bought off with two bottles of iodine, a dozen aspirin, or in exceptional cases, a roll of adhesive tape.

When the Derrick Brothers refused Nady's request to open a branch clinic under his own management, he secured a five-hundred dollar loan from Becky's secret bank account and entered a partnership with a physician and a friend to start a new office. One day the new entrepreneur had a setback when a rival solicitor paraded past his window with one of his medicine cabinets. That afternoon, Nady received a telephone call that made him forget the slight. Slamming down the receiver, his face turned white and then burnt red.

"They hit my father!" he stammered.

Company goons had beaten union loyalist Barnett at the shop.

Nady's mind flashed to Barnett's utter weariness after a day at the steam iron, the lines on his face that were getting deeper, and his sagging shoulders.

"I'm going!" he snapped without fanfare.

Speeding out the door, he caught sight of his pal Murray following along with a hammer tucked into his waist.

Within minutes, Nady had kicked in the office door of Barnett's workplace and burst into the showroom.

"Who hit my father? Who hit my father?" his maniacal voice kept repeating.

A paunch-bellied, cigar chomping, thuggish character immediately stepped forward.

"I did—what of it?" he boasted.

Without a second thought, Nady swung blindly, crushing the man's nose.

He could barely hear the chaotic ring of his shouts and curses amid the crash of splintering glass and overturned chairs and tables.

When the assault was over and his energy spent, Nady found himself pinned against a wall by a huge and unfriendly bald man.

Just as he began to reassess the wisdom of the entire episode, Murray came to the rescue. A series of well-placed hammer strokes at the back of the bald man's head did the trick.

Racing out the door, the duo found a waiting elevator full of passengers frozen in silent fear.

"Get going fast!" Nady ordered the car's operator, borrowing a favorite line from the movies.

As the two outlaws melted into the stream of Seventh Avenue pushcarts and pedestrians, they could hear the wail of approaching sirens.

Shirt-ripped and bloodied, Becky's younger son arrived at home to face the wrath of his mother. Yet poor Barnett was the real target of her rage.

"Go, start with de bosses," she chastised.

"He coulda got killed.... All de gangsters in the woild, the whole woild, was in dot shop!"

Becky then ordered her son to stay away from home for three days. Meanwhile, she approached intermediaries to assure the mob that her son "dint mean nottin'!"

When Nady returned, his mother found ninety dollars to rent a room for the summer at Rockaway Beach, a working-class Atlantic Ocean resort easily reached by subway. On weekends, Barnett could soak his aching feet in the healing salt water, and available cots could accommodate a variety of visiting aunts, uncles, and cousins. Most of all, Becky had provided her son a welcome refuge from the feared vengeance of the garment trade racketeers.

Redemption

Seeking to escape the seediness of the worker's compensation racket, Nady took to regular handball sessions at Castle Hill Park in the East Bronx. On weekends, he often hiked from the end of the trolley line north of Manhattan's Washington Heights and caught the Dyckman Street ferry across the Harlem River to the North Bronx. Scaling the Palisades overlooking the Hudson and reveling in the unspoiled natural scenery, he liked to remove his shirt on the long walk to Yonkers and back home. Meanwhile, Nady continued to find time for the output of poems, short stories, and plays that would mark his entire adult life. One Bronx dialect piece, "Subway Sarah," offered a confessional monologue of a lowly and lonesome office worker riding home after a long day at the job.

In 1933, not long after the Horowitz family moved to a new apartment just west of the upscale Grand Concourse, Barnett quietly sobbed as Teddy cleaned out her closet. She was about to marry Bernie Mass, an amiable fellow she had me at a Catskill hotel the previous summer. Teddy had once aroused the interest of the young actor, Jack Albertson, but an ever-vigilant Becky had squelched any chance of a liaison with a man of the theater. In contrast, Bernie and his brother, also named Teddy, were the sons of a construction contractor and his Hungarian wife. Two years later, Becky rented a summer bungalow at Lake Huntington, a modest resort on the southwestern edge of the Catskills, where Teddy could recover from a miscarriage while her husband and his brother commuted on weekends.

When the Mass Brothers asked Nady to come along in mid-June, he declined. Following a new state law prohibiting solicitations for worker's compensation cases, he was jobless once more. Yet as temperatures soared days later, Bernie and Teddy waved a pair of handball gloves in front of his face.

"Waddya wanna sweat your galloons off for?" Ted Mass implored.

Minutes later the threesome set off for the Catskills in Bernie's Ford sedan. The trip would provide a life-defining experience for the lanky Bronxite.

2

DOROTHY'S DREAMS

Immediately after arriving at Lake Huntington, Nady raced down to the rowboat Bernie Mass had rented. As the New York exile pulled the dinghy from the shore, he found himself so overwhelmed by the scene that he stripped down to his underwear and leaped into the waters.

"Cold, isn't it?" he heard a voice cry out as he retreated to the warmth of the beach.

Broadway Casino

A young, dark-skinned woman with a high forehead and almond eyes regarded him in studied contemplation. She was eighteen-year-old Dorothy Levine, out fishing with the kosher butcher's daughter. As the beauty on the beach engaged him in intellectual and political banter, the twenty-six-year-old, dark haired, curly-topped unmarried pipe smoker sensed he was over-matched. His only recourse was to challenge her to race to the other side of the lake.

When Nady approached the opposite shore, a quarter of a mile away, he interrupted his spastic stroking to look behind to where his competitor might be.

To his wonderment, he saw no one.

Instead, the stranger sat patiently on the beach ahead of him.

"Let's swim back," she proposed cheerfully as he emerged from the icy waters, desperate to catch his breath and rest his aching arms.

Later that evening, Nady and the crew ended up at Nat Levine's Broadway Casino—the closest Lake Huntington came to a pleasure palace. Outdoor placards advertised "Chow Mein, Chop Suey, Dining, Dancing, Beer on Draught, Hot Dogs, 'Phillies' Cigars, Soda, Ice Cream, Candy, Boats to Let," as well as an outdoor Pavilion. Inside, the bar and dance hall featured the Harlem jazz of the Eddie White Combo and offered one free whiskey for every three bought.

Dorothy, the proprietor's daughter, was the sole cocktail server, a task she added to summer stints as breakfast and lunch chef, boat concessionaire, and purveyor of malteds, ice cream, popcorn, and cigarettes. Before Prohibition's repeal in 1933, she had served bootleg whiskey in tea cups and kept an eye out for the police. Nady found himself completely captivated by the young woman's penetrating glance and the way her suntanned skin played off against her black uniform and white lace fringe. The drinks were robust that night, and he won the house raffle, a promising sign since for the first time in his rather protected life, he had fallen in love.

He made sure his party left a generous thirty-five cent tip.

The Levines

From Nady Horowitz's perspective, the seemingly acculturated Levines were practically Yankees, but their story was only a slightly more upscale version of his own family saga.

Dorothy's father, Nathan, (originally Nassan Liebenkraft), born in 1891, was the youngest son of a Jewish family of professional musicians from the Belorussian city of Minsk. Escaping the draft at age fourteen during the Russo-Japanese War of 1905, he migrated to America carrying only a battered suitcase and a mandolin. Taken in by cousins in the Ft. Hamilton section of Brooklyn, he completed high school and went to work in his relatives' Lower East Side restaurant.

Waitress Bessie Hertzig, an immigrant from the southwestern Polish town of Lemberg, took notice of the dark, handsome newcomer. The Hertzig family, including two sons and five daughters, had come to New York around 1895. Bess fostered no sentimentality about the Old Country, often referring to her kinsfolk as "a pack of horse thieves." She bitterly remembered how older siblings had dragged her from school for beatings and a return to work at the family shop. Once Nathan and Bess married in 1912, they settled on the Lower East Side, where Nathan entered succeeding partnerships in a Broome Street delicatessen and a restaurant on Lower Broadway. Within a year of the wedding, they had a son, Milton David, followed by Dorothy, born on February 15, 1917, the day after St. Valentine's Day.

Legend held that a neighbor jokingly advised Bess to leave the anemic and jaundiced infant at the hospital.

Not long after Nathan received his citizenship papers in 1920, the Levines moved to the South Bronx, where each room had windows for light and fresh air and the apartment boasted a private bathroom. Later in the decade, the building's coin-operated gas lamps would give way to electric lighting. The family lived on Bryant Avenue, a street containing two apartment houses, several private dwellings, a row of older brownstone residences, two family-run stores, and an empty lot. Most relatives were within walking distance. Neighbors included a mix of Orthodox Jews, barely observant brethren, and a few agnostic socialists, including the downstairs tenant, the treasurer of the Amalgamated Clothing Workers.

Milton and Dorothy shared a pleasant childhood that included visits to the public library, adventures at the local coal yard, sidewalk roller-skating sessions, trips to the Bronx Zoo, and occasional excursions to Yankee Stadium to cheer on Babe Ruth. An inveterate tomboy, Dorothy had a reputation for a mean curve ball. Meanwhile, she and her brother accompanied their parents to neighborhood theater performances, vaudeville shows, and movie houses. When the two saved their pennies to purchase a ticket to Sigmund Romberg's operetta, *The New Moon*, as a Mother's Day gift, Milt walked home from midtown Manhattan because the price of admission left no change for subway fare.

The Levine offspring often engaged in spirited competitions over who could get the furthest on a single subway fare. They also "played school" because Dorothy loved to recite her classroom lessons and read dramatic excerpts, particularly those associated with Broadway star Ethel Barrymore. After the family acquired a radio in the mid-Twenties, announcers and performers took on an intimate familiarity. Yet the appeal of modern popular culture had its limits. When Bess followed flapper fashion by cutting her long hair and "bobbing" it, her stunned husband would not talk to her for weeks.

The most exciting family adventures surrounded Nat Levine's driving. In 1919, he joined two partners in investing in a new Ford Model T with a crank starter. After mastering the technique of putting the vehicle into motion, he managed to crash into an elevated subway pillar, mount the raised tracks of a trolley line before confronting an advancing train, and lose control when racing another driver, causing the car to veer off the street, hit the sidewalk, and turn over completely. Amazingly, no one ever was hurt in these mishaps. Nathan's business acumen was no less legendary. His record included a failed deli and partnership in a doomed Lower East Side restaurant. This may explain that while anticipating a position as night manager of an East Broadway eatery, he rejected a proposal from a fellow waiter named Lindenbaum to go in as partners in an uptown bistro.

That establishment later became Lindy's, the café of choice for the Broadway theater crowd and the home of the most famous cheesecake in the world.

Bess Levine's outlet was the Socialist Party. Serving as a poll watcher for its 1920 presidential candidate, Eugene Debs, she became a regular delegate to party conventions and raised funds to help organize mill workers, miners, and southern sharecroppers. Yet Nat Levine continued to foster entrepreneurial aspirations. In 1926, the former waiter bought a Chinese restaurant in Honesdale, a small industrial town in Pennsylvania's Pocono Mountains. The family roomed in a bleak Main Street rental that perennially smelled of chili beans and onions from the Texas hotdog shop below. With a population of some eight thousand, Honesdale boasted only one other Jewish family—the operators of the town's main factory and largest department store. Aside from the Irish-Catholic minority, most of the residents were evangelical Protestants. On their second night in town, the Levines witnessed a parade of thousands of cross-carrying, anti-Catholic and anti-Semitic Ku Klux Klansmen in town for a statewide "klonvocation."

Milton easily made common cause with working-class Irish mates at school, who bestowed him the nickname of "Mickey" as a sign of acceptance, one he would use in years to come. Elected Freshman Class President, the outgoing New Yorker thrived despite occasional bursts of hostility from Protestant locals. Yet the restaurant failed in 1927 and the Levines relocated their summer business to Lake Huntington. For the next several years, Milt and Dorothy left school early in late May to lend their hands to the operation. Meanwhile, they accompanied Bess to Socialist events such as the rally at the Bronx Coliseum featuring the new party leader, former Presbyterian minister Norman Thomas.

The Socialists insisted that the prosperity of the Twenties was built on a house of cards and that capitalism was about to undergo its final crisis. Apparently, Nat Levine knew better. Ignoring his wife's warnings, he followed an insider's tip that the post-1929 collapse in stock prices was temporary and invested most of the family savings in the Irving Trust Company.

The stock market value of the doomed financial institution quickly plunged from seventy-eight to two dollars a share.

Not long after, the Levines used connections in the Socialist movement to garner a place in the Amalgamated Clothing Workers cooperative housing project in the North Bronx. Situated near spacious Van Cortland Park, the nine "garden apartment" buildings offered four sunlit and airy rooms with exposures in four directions. The community's social life included tenant meetings and an array of seminars, socialist lectures, debates, and free concerts.

Spurred by Bess's determination to see her children educated, Milt ignored his father's ridicule and enrolled at tuition-free City College, at that point, a predominantly working-class Jewish institution. Yet the radical political dialectics of the student cafeteria "alcoves" intimidated him, compelling him to confine his intellectual growth to reading hundreds of plays. After graduating with a lackluster record in 1934, Milt remained jobless until a friend secured him a sixteen-dollar-a-week position as a retail clerk during the Christmas rush. Bess cried when her son brought home his first paycheck, despairing that a college degree meant nothing more than a place in the stockroom. Weeks later, her brother Charlie Hertzig came to the rescue.

If Bess's brand of immigrant Judaism centered on social justice and radical politics, Charlie's desire to live the American Dream led to a fabulously successful entrepreneurial career. Working as a newsboy in the first years of the century, Hertzig teamed up with four cohorts to form the Metropolitan News Company of New York. The combine prospered by hand-delivering four Yiddish dailies to Lower East Side pushcart vendors and servicing the uptown trade by horse and wagon. Once Hertzig assumed control of the enterprise, it became the largest newspaper wholesaler in the nation, permitting its owner to invest in an empire of hotels, restaurants, nursing homes, bowling alleys, movie palaces, and theaters. A soft touch for Bess's requests for financial contributions to socialist or humanitarian causes, "Uncle Charlie" now hired his nephew as "assistant treasurer" or cashier for one of his newly acquired Depression-immune investments—a Minsky's burlesque house in Brooklyn.

A World to Win

While Milt's prospects seemed unclear, Dorothy prospered. Enrolled at Prospect Junior High, she won the *New York Times* Best School Orator Prize of 1930 for a speech on the Constitution entitled "The Birth of America." At the same time, she produced a volume of introspective verse she called "Inspired in Winter"—dedicated to "friends who belong to my surroundings." One of her poems fantasized about being the "lover, advisor, and friend" of her civics teacher. In contrast, "An Unemployed (Dedicated to Charly on 183rd Street)" presented a free verse portrait of a Depression apple vendor. "By the Lake," a volume assembled in 1931, described quiet moments of solitude away from family and the Lake Huntington cabaret.

Once at Walton High School, Dorothy struck up a life-long friendship with intellectual cohorts Pat Wexler and Laura Gilman and began dating the dapper Rube Cheroff. Joining the Dramatic Club and yearbook staff, she won election to student government and the Honor Society. Meanwhile, she threw herself into a variety of creative writing and verse.

The wistful poem, "My Past," pretends to chronicle haunting memories:

> ... a past lover, an affair, scenes,
> Ambitions, ideals, lordly schemes

"Hope" speaks to the loneliness of an adolescent dreamer:

> I grasp it hungrily,
> I grasp it desperately,
> Wishing in vain, waiting.
> Wishing again, debating.
> Tearful, fearful – hesitating.
> Hope, I need you urgently.
> I pray to you fervently.
> I am your slave.

Another verse, "Middle Lines (1935)," offers the tender reverie of a seventeen-year-old:

> Oh, my lover, my lonely lovely lover,
> Rather ask
> How many trees in all these woods
> Or the count of threads in my bride gown of lace,
> Never— how many kisses on an August day!

Dorothy's most ambitious project, a romantic political novella entitled "They Have a World to Win," expropriated a phrase from Karl Marx's *Communist Manifesto* for the title.

Rescue

About to start her second year studying journalism at Hunter College, New York's tuition-free institution for women, Dorothy used Nady's weekend visits to treat him to ongoing tutorials on the Levines and Lake

Huntington. Situated in a remote corner of the Catskills, the resort had flourished in the late 1920s and early Thirties as a vacation spot for a "fast" crowd of New York Jews, attracting the attention of the Ku Klux Klan. At its peak, the town boasted a summer population over five thousand, ten hotels serving three hundred guests each, a host of bungalow colonies, three kosher butchers, a huge dance hall—the Nutshell House—as well as three thriving "casinos." "Nat Levine's" was located in a run-down two-story clapboard structure on the lakefront. Dealt a reputation as one of the community's more marginal establishments (the local priest denounced the saloon so that parishioners would patronize an Irish-Catholic rival), the seedy facility substituted innovation for respectability.

Nat and Bess responded to these challenges by introducing what locals remember as the first Chinese cuisine in Sullivan County. They even hired a Chinese chef, although his notorious drinking resulted in frequent absences. When necessity required Bess to fill in at the grill, Dorothy had strict orders to call out orders to "Chan." According to old-timers, the Levines brought the first black jazz bands to the county in the late Twenties. As a youngster, Dorothy danced the Charleston for customers. Through the end of Prohibition in 1933, moreover, the Broadway Casino was one of the few places in Lake Huntington to serve bootleg whiskey. During raids, young Dorothy had the responsibility of hiding the contraband.

To round out the picture, the Casino's upstairs level hosted illegal gambling. Local legend holds that on several occasions Nat Levine and Milt received advance warning of state police visits and tossed the slot machines into the lake. A dredging operation in the late-1990s discovered some of the equipment irretrievably submerged beneath the waters.

Somewhat intimidated by the worldly and agnostic Levines, Nady sensed that Dorothy's father questioned the manhood of any suitor who did not guzzle whiskey or wolf down pork, ham, or Chow Mein. Dorothy responded by describing Bess's unhappiness with the environment of a glorified country saloon. She also hinted how her father's shiny black hair and olive skin frequently appealed to female admirers, even married ones. Dorothy insisted on leading her beau past the superficial charms of the lake community.

"Wake up, Nady, look at what's happening around you!" she prodded.

A fierce desire to cleanse the world compelled this Lake Huntington princess to detail the moral hypocrisies of local churchgoers and assorted drunks such as the parish priest, not to mention the inevitable lake drowning accidents occurring every season. Perhaps she saw the barely educated, naive, and unemployed poet as a project she could fashion into the savior who could deliver her from the seediness and apparent hopelessness of her surroundings.

Whatever the case, the summer of 1935 brought an unlikely but torrid love affair between the dreamy eighteen-year-old and the pipe-smoking romantic nearly nine years her senior she now addressed as "Nat."

"I have such infinite tenderness for you," Dorothy wrote to him one week.

"We'll take the last bus back Sunday so that we can kiss from Wurtsboro to Kingsbridge Road," she promised as they planned a return to the city at the close of a weekend.

Another letter compared her love for the lanky Bronxite to the "impetuous and unassuming" burst of thunder that recently had shaken the resort's foundations.

"If you only knew how much I wanted to believe in you," she confided.

"I can't forgive you for being human, moral,—and fallible. I believe I hate you for being a reality. You have compelled me to stop pretending, to stop playing."

In "A Sonnet to You," Dorothy acknowledged the depth of her feelings:

> Ah, love me not for thine own vanity,
> But try to think of soul and heart and mind.
> Your love provokes such sweet insanity
> I fear my senses I shall never find.

One notation took notice of the concern that she was too young for him.

"Perhaps, as you say, Nat, I love you too impulsively, or in a youthful manner," Dorothy conceded.

Yet she coupled this with an insistence that "I love you so much in spite of your accent on my youth. There is nothing to fear."

Star-Crossed

As the school year resumed in the fall of 1935, Nat and Bess Levine left for Miami Beach, where Charlie Hertzig had hired his brother-in-law as manager of Minsky's Burlesque on South Pier. Dorothy stayed with family friends in the Bronx to continue her studies at Hunter. When she developed a nagging cough that winter, however, she took a term's leave of absence to convalesce down South. Although socialists viewed burlesque as the epitome of capitalist decadence, Dorothy admired entertainers such as vaudeville perennial, Sophie Tucker, and strip-tease artist, Gypsy Rose Lee—a part-time novelist and painter known as the "elegant lady." She soon took to composing letters for several dancers, who reciprocated by teaching the "College Virgin" trade secrets, including the knack of twirling their provocatively placed tassels in opposite directions.

The experience inspired a new play. "Parisian Burlesque: A Cross Section In One Short Scene" describes a chorus girl who prevails upon a street-wise producer to incorporate the melodies of a serious young musician with whom she has fallen in love.

"Nat—I don't believe in 'Art' or 'Realism' or 'Romanticism,'" Dorothy explained.

"This is a new school of writing: 'Recordivism.'"

Whatever Miami's inspirations, Dorothy missed her young man in the Bronx.

"Darling, don't feel depressed," she wrote, "you're not completely alone because I'm always with you. I want to mean everything to you. I want to be your Poetry, your idealism, your Hopes, and your Happiness. Do you think I can?"

"You probably realize by now that I love you sincerely—and completely," she persisted. "Yet, in spite of the apparent futility of our situation, I want you to love me—at least until I come back to your arms in April."

As Dorothy's nineteenth birthday approached, she assumed a worldly approach to the romance that belied her age and inexperience. She hoped that once she returned to New York,

> both of us will have a much more mature and hopeful attitude towards all things. I ask you to find a new faith in the things that will come, that must come, because we are young. I refuse to believe in the destiny that must separate us. And I do again refuse to believe in anything that permits another man to be as intimate with me as you have been.

Despite Dorothy's desires, the paths of the two lovers seemed to be proceeding in different directions. By the spring of 1936, Barnett and Becky Horowitz had moved to a new Bronx apartment on Walton Avenue. With his personal relationship as a lodestar, Nady now sought to market creative works such as "Yellow as Gold, a Basketball Story" under the pseudonym "Nick Harris," an early use of the last name brother Sam brought back from the Marines. He also entered into a partnership with Mike Kanin. Painting the backdrop for a burlesque theater, Mike had suffered a detached retina when a falling piece of scenery struck his face. The hospital bandages covering the patient's eyes reduced Nady to tears. Once discharged, Mike abandoned his art career and agreed to team up with his friend to write plays and sketches.

After making some changes to "Burn the Wheat," one of Nady's single-act dramas from the early Thirties, the duo tasted a degree of success when the piece made the finals of a competition held by *Stage* magazine. Other collaborations included the political "Bryant Park," a sketch depicting the disaffection of unemployed men, vagrants, and prostitutes rotting away on benches behind the New York Public Library. The sentimental "Strip-Tease," in turn, depicted an exotic dancer's affection for a member of a college crew team.

Switching to a movie script, Kanin and "Nat Harris" came up with "Hi Diddle Diddle"—a comic extravaganza about a newspaper clerk accidentally propelled to aviator stardom. The farce included a pastel colored "Moon sequence," a reflection of Nady's longtime fascination with science fiction, and a scene with "Harlemesque" figures conversing in Negro dialect. "Willy Nilly: A New Revue," designated "for stage and screen," centered on two writers who create a complete production in rhyme, an artifice that extends to lobby billboards, theater signs, program notes, and intermission announcements—even the jingles pumped into the men's restroom.

Through their manic playfulness with words and energetic embrace of popular culture, Kanin and Harris seemed to be willing their way past the restricted opportunities of the stagnant economy and their marginalized status as working-class Jews. Yet Nady could not help anguishing over the paucity of prospects for supporting himself. Accordingly, just as Dorothy prepared to return from Miami, he left for New Bedford to work at the food market his Aunt Eva and Uncle Nathan ran. Yet the venture proved disappointing. Baffled by the Portuguese accents of the store's clientele, unfamiliar with local produce, and unenthusiastic about plans to set him up in the retail clothing business, he was back in the Bronx by

May. By then, however, Dorothy had relocated for the summer to Lake Huntington, whose modestly priced amenities continued to afford some protection from the Depression's impact on the tourist trade.

"What a village," she wrote. "Everyone is building, expanding, enlarging, and competing with his neighbor. How pathetic—this grappling for the much coveted dollar."

A second letter offered a more personal touch.

"Now I know definitely," Dorothy bravely announced, "I can't be without you this summer. That I know as well as the contours in your delightfully virile and youthful body."

Another note proposed that the two rendezvous in New York for an all-Wagner Sunday concert at City College or an evening debate between socialists Upton Sinclair and Norman Thomas. On second thought, Dorothy suggested a visit to the Planetarium or a walk.

The Lure of Celluloid

In a quandary over the improbable relationship and anxious to prove himself as a creative force, Nady announced during Thanksgiving of 1936 that he was leaving for Los Angeles to seek his fortune in the movies—a fascination nurtured since childhood. Lou, a basketball teammate, planned to drive to the Coast with his brother-in-law and sought a third rider to share expenses. Nady Horowitz, now Nat Harris, saw Hollywood as the land of opportunity where the barely educated and seasoned son of immigrants could win acceptance as the writer he hoped to be. After all, screenwriter Moss Hart, Metro-Goldwyn-Mayer (MGM) studio head Dore Schary, and Paramount Pictures chief Don Hartman all had begun their careers as Catskill Mountain social directors, and New York Jews from vaudeville and Broadway dominated the movie colony.

Barnett trembled as Nady prepared to leave on December 1st. As Lou drove up, Becky clung to her son. For her part, Dorothy was coldly silent as she kissed the man in her life good-bye. Once on the road, the aspiring screenwriter recorded his impressions in a school notebook that he called *California Log – A Chronicle of Unimportance – the adventures of three Bronx boys and a transcontinental tour.* The journal included descriptions of the swamps of New Jersey, the frozen Susquehanna River, somber Gettysburg, Virginia tobacco fields, the grandeur of the Appalachian Mountains, Negro huts in the Arkansas cotton fields, a carnival in

Texarkana, cowboys west of Ft. Worth, the oil rigs of Odessa and Midland, Indian grass huts in Arizona's Gila Valley, and the impressive Boulder Dam. It was the Grand Canyon, however, that elicited the author's most heartfelt response.

"My eyes have seen glory," Nady exuded, a prelude to a reflection on the relative grandeur of Nature and Man he would engage in repeatedly over time.

"My infinitesimal worth is impressed on me," he wrote. "I know now, where I believed before, that I am not even a mere fly."

As the trio approached Los Angeles, Nady offered a hopeful prayer.

"We don't know what lies before us," he mused. "We only know that we are young, eager, and able. Opportunity, should it come, will find us prepared."

Such evocations of the American Dream, however, contrasted with the cheap burlesque and movie houses, second hand clothing shops, traffic congestion, noise, and dirty slums of downtown Los Angeles reminiscent of Manhattan's 14th Street. Besides, the would-be writer's ticket of entry to movie land did not exactly open doors. Garson Kanin, who had moved from burlesque comedy to the Broadway stage and established contacts in Hollywood, had prevailed upon comic screenwriter Sam Spewack to provide Nady a letter of introduction to an executive at Republic Productions, a recently formed studio specializing in "B" westerns and action films.

"Here's a young man—Nat Harris," wrote Spewack, "who writes lyrics as well as stories and who is a friend of a friend of mine."

"He would like to get a hearing and a reading. He has some material, and he is primarily interested in either selling it, or getting a job, or both."

Breaking into Hollywood proved far more difficult than imagined. One day Nady managed to stumble into the private office of a studio boss "measuring" the bust of a blonde beauty. On another, he wound up having an afternoon drink with screen celebrities Victor Moore and Helen Broderick, who offhandedly thanked him when he treated them to refills. On another occasion, the actor George Raft reprimanded him for nearly denting the fender of his car while Nat ran some errands in Lou's sedan. Meanwhile, his pal's chronic bouts of stomach pain developed into a ruptured appendix, prompting relatives in New York to wire hundreds of dollars so that Nady could arrange for hospitalization and daily updates on the patient's condition.

"Should it ever be possible to reciprocate for all that you are doing," Lou's brother wrote, "rest assured that you can absolutely depend upon me."

Following instructions, Nady eventually placed the recovered patient on a train back East. By the spring of 1937, however, it was clear that the aspiring dramatist had missed the opportunity to make an impression in movie-land, if such a prospect had been possible for an unpolished author of dialect sketches and farcical extravaganzas who lacked sufficient self-confidence to sell himself. Besides, the transplanted New Yorker missed his family, longed for the familiar environs of home, and wondered about his dark-haired sweetheart.

Dialectics

The prodigal son returned by rail just in time for Passover Seder in the Bronx. Nearly twenty-nine years of age without any prospects, Nady wasted no time in contacting Lou's relatives for an anticipated position in the family hat company. In standing by his pal, however, he had ignored one of Becky's most well-chosen words of advice.

"Don't go so overboard for your friends," his mother liked to say in Yiddish, a warning that conveyed the foolishness of expecting even close pals to reciprocate acts of generosity.

When all the members of Lou's family seemed to be "very busy," therefore, Nady was not completely surprised. Yet the experience would offer a prime example of what he often referred to as life's "hard knocks," contributing to a lingering cynicism about the world beyond the home. Ignored in Hollywood and rebuffed in New York, the unemployed Bronx adventurer once again set out for New Bedford to explore prospects. When he returned, however, Dorothy was spending Easter vacation with her parents in Miami.

During Nat's sojourn to Hollywood, Dorothy Levine had expanded upon her writing efforts. A proto-feminist play, "Love Is Not Love," describes the attempts of an alluring young woman painter to win respect for her contributions to art. Another, "The Rape of the Sabine Women," prepared for a classics class and dedicated to best friend Pat Wexler, alters the theme of the famous painting to suggest that its female victims planned their submission to the Roman conquerors to perpetuate the tribe when the Sabine men lost interest in propagation and became indifferent to their charms.

"Polyphonic Thoughts on My Twentieth Birthday," a poem written in February 1937, mixes romantic anguish with a dose of Depression realism:

> Living is a tearful torment,
> And this subtle substance
> Men call a soul
> Is seething with suppression.
>
> . . . .
> I would be done with this weary world
> That wears its gay colors
> O'er a rotten core
> Like any other street whore.

The political subtext of Dorothy's writing stemmed from a recent affiliation with the Young People's Socialist League (YPSL), a youth group of socialist revolutionaries who supported Leon Trotsky, the former Red Army leader and dissident exiled in 1929 by Soviet leader Joseph Stalin. She also embraced Trotsky's critique of the Soviet dictatorship by following Milt into the Workers Party, a mainstay of the "old man's" Fourth International. Both Levines now met fundraising quotas and hawked copies of the *Militant* newspaper while Dorothy served as the "reasonable" voice at street-corner rallies. By her own admission, her good looks often attracted young men to the cause.

Dorothy's poem, "A Dream of Greatness," sought to express her political aspirations:

> But even with the smell of death in his face,
> Man found himself a new idea, a new life.
> No more war, no more hunger, no more misery,
> Man found himself....
>
> . . . .
> Go, Man, see for yourselves, once more and the last time,
> And inherit the Universe.

Building on her literary and political endeavors, the newborn Trotskyist began to proselytize her working-class wordsmith from the

Bronx. One letter to California reported on a YPSL meeting centered on the "gruesome" plight of southern sharecroppers. Then she boasted she had "converted" someone into joining the radical Lawyers Guild and Socialist Party.

"You're next, Nat," Dorothy proclaimed in half-jest.

The Bronxite had "the temperament for an A-one radical," she explained, because he was Jewish, a proletarian, and an intelligent, sensitive author of "class struggle plays."

Nevertheless, she would not see him for weeks. Days before Nat returned from California, Dorothy took the train to Miami to spend another Easter break with her parents, where she felt increasingly isolated.

"You go to a movie, and people actually *applaud* [Italian fascist dictator] Mussolini and believe [industrial union] sit-down strikes are mob rule," she complained.

"Everything is bottled up inside of me. Don't you see, Nat, the 'cause' is part of me, actually, and everything that happens to me is analyzed in terms of the 'class struggle.'"

Dorothy confided that Miami's luxurious homes, Packard automobiles, thousand-dollar racing bets, and rampant drunkenness led to her feeling depressed and helpless.

"I must do something about it all," she exclaimed.

"Nat, there are so many things to be done."

Upon his return from California, a second letter from Miami addressed the aspiring writer as "my poor comrade." It began with an appeal to Nathan's Jewish sensibilities.

"Jesus was a nincompoop," Dorothy proclaimed:

> He saw abuses, yes, and wanted to reform the world, so he called himself the Son of God, meaning the Son of a non-existent Being, and turned the other cheek. That was silly of him. He should have led his band of lusty revolutionary Jews with the determination of a Moses, the cunning of a David, and stormed the holy synagogue where the High Priests dominated every Jew in the community with a rigid hand. He should have kicked these Jewish landlords of God in the pants, and set up his new, more equitable society.

"Need I continue the analogy," Dorothy could not resist adding, "to state that our laborers today are being crucified on the cross of capitalism."

From there, the author redirected her focus to the reader, who apparently had difficulty wading through the political material she had forwarded.

"And you!" she admonished. "You exasperate me. But you can't help it! You've been brought up with the pernicious capitalistic propaganda since you were old enough to read editorials on why Russia won't succeed."

Dorothy now responded to the charge that socialists misread human nature. "What is sacred human nature?" she asked. Was it natural, she persisted, for children to slave in southern cotton mills, for undernourished sharecroppers "to grovel in tin-can shacks," for twelve million people to parade in the streets in search of $12 a week jobs?

"It is the *present* system that is against 'human nature,'" Dorothy protested. "Marx merely translates this feeling of injustice into sound economic theory."

Fearful that she may have pushed Nady too far, she confessed she was not angry with him, just impatient. "Please read the other pamphlets," Dorothy pleaded. "I admit they're tough, but see what you can do with them for my sake."

"Remember," she admonished, the average weekly wage in the United States was $17.98 while the Morgans and Hearsts stored "countless millions."

"Nat, will you march on May 1?" the letter concluded, a reference to the labor movement's traditional day of solidarity.

An Unlikely Union

A subsequent note from Miami asked if the radical posturing of her earlier missive had made Nat angry.

"I was so enraged," confessed Dorothy, "I should have written everything off my chest, and then thrown the letter away."

Indeed, much of the Florida correspondence addressed Dorothy's complicated and often contradictory feelings for her beau and their prospects for marriage. One note described a romantic reverie on a park bench.

"I forgot the 'masses' for two split hours," Dorothy reported, "and became a smug prig not caring a fig for the pigs of society."

"I love you so much, I want to do everything you ask of me," she wrote on another occasion.

"Nat, we're a couple of dreamy tin-can poets. And I promise to love you always, and obey you—sometimes."

Nevertheless, Dorothy sensed Nathan's reluctance to commit to marriage as long as he was out of work.

"I want to be your wife, whether you want to be my husband or not," she insisted. At the same time, Dorothy had her own misgivings.

"Darling, forgive me," she wrote from Miami,

> I've lost my good humor, because I've been desolately alone, and more lonely than I would be without my parents. You know how things are with them, ... Well, it's quite distasteful to me—not only as an observer, but as a daughter. So if my ideas are warped on marriage, you understand why.

Even before Dorothy returned to New York, Nat was back in New Bedford with the apparent understanding that a successful job search would allow the couple to marry.

"I'm so glad your relatives are decent folk," she wrote.

"Honey, I'd hate to introduce you to my pack of wolves. That's why I want to run off and get married. I'm afraid to start out fresh under their bushy eyebrows."

At the same time, Dorothy worried about her intended husband's family.

"Nat, are you sure you told your mother we want to get married?" she asked.

"Perhaps it's my intuitive soul, but I don't think your mother is at all enthusiastic or happy about it. Are you, darling? ... Think now, honey, in the calm of Bedford before you come to the cataclysm of the Bronx."

When Nat announced he was leaving New Bedford without prospects, Dorothy took that to mean there would be no September wedding as planned.

"I know we'll be happy, if we only get a tiny decent start," she proclaimed.

"But, chances look glum, don't they?"

Throughout the courtship, Dorothy insisted that Nathan refrain from giving her any presents until he found work. At the same time, she tried to navigate around his "unemployment problem." "I'm afraid you're much too interested in making money," she advised from Miami:

If it's for me—and I don't think so—you remember what I told you. I'm not interested in a "snappy ultra-streamlined" apartment for our friends to dump cigarette ashes within; not do I want a $500 fur coat, ...new Plymouths—nor Miami winter siestas—nor rocks (the expensive kind) or any of the other bourgeois paraphernalia.

Dorothy then spelled out her domestic dream:

I want a small clean apartment with plenty of air and space for its environs. I want a job. I want you to have a more secure one, though. I want to save for our children's education. And I want to see two plays a month, and at least one concert...and I want to read loads of books, attend infinite mass meetings—and in between make potential Roberts with you and love you till you raise the white flag. And we could do that on thirty a week, couldn't we?

Sometime during the fall of 1937, Nat bought the restaurant cloakroom concession from Charlie Hertzig, who claimed to have taken a liking to the young man. The couple now planned a February wedding for the month after Dorothy's graduation. Although class valedictorian, however, the graduate never attended the commencement for political reasons. On Columbus Day, she had joined a small contingent of Trotskyists picketing a march of five thousand followers of the Roman Catholic fraternal order, the Knights of Columbus, who were using the event to honor Italian fascist Benito Mussolini. Only the quick action of several Irish-American police officers, who hustled the young protester to the safety of a nearby subway entrance, had likely prevented her from physical harm. Dorothy's boycott of graduation reflected her disillusionment over the Hunter College faculty's refusal to take a stand on the threat of fascism and Hitlerism as the world careened toward war. She expressed these views in the January 1938 edition of *Echo*, the college literary magazine.

"When a bourgeois-democracy with its police system and parliamentary hypocrisies can no longer check the masses of the impoverished workers, the unemployed, and when there is a possibility of the masses establishing a workers' state," she proclaimed in boilerplate Marxist jargon, "the bourgeoisie plays its last card—Fascism."

Fascist dictatorship, Dorothy concluded, was "the hypodermic administered to the diseased and senile capitalist system."

Although Nathan seemed to show little interest in, never mind comprehension, of such rhetoric, he nevertheless appeared to Dorothy as a worthy deliverer from the seediness of Lake Huntington, her parents' domestic difficulties, and the seeming hopelessness of the times. Regardless of his uncertain financial status, the diamond in the rough from the Bronx was her project and she had immense faith in him as a writer, human being, and lover.

Nat, in turn, worshiped the beautiful and commanding young woman and poet who insisted against all logic that she wanted to spend the rest of her life with him. Given the eight-and-a-half-year difference in age, distinct family backgrounds, contrary religious views, and disparate political philosophies, however, he could not help but see himself as a poor match.

Unsure of the pair's ultimate compatibility or his suitability for marriage, the prospective groom sought advice on a long walk with musician friend Charles Kingsford.

"Charlie, I'm getting married," Nathan announced. "How it will work out, I don't know. I have some doubts—I'm a nut, and she's just too damned bright—her parents expected someone better."

"Well," Charlie responded in the spirit of the cultural avant-garde, "nothing is forever."

"If it doesn't go," Kingsford shrugged after a pause, "you'll just break it up."

3

BRONX TALES

Charlie Kingsford wound up playing the wedding march for the ceremony. Once a rabbi presided over the exchange of vows, one hundred guests partook of a sit-down banquet courtesy of the Levines. The only interruption in the proceedings came in the form of loudspeaker announcements updating the match between heavyweights Joe Louis and Jack Braddock. Charlie Hertzig blessed the couple with a $150 gift.

Tender Comrades

Nathan and Dorothy spent their wedding night at a hotel on Manhattan's Upper West Side, selected by the groom for its indoor handball court. Two well-dressed young women in high heels eyed the lanky newlywed in the lobby but lost interest when they discovered the purpose of his stay. Once Nat relinquished the coatroom lease a month later, he and Dorothy caught the train for a Miami Beach honeymoon.

Demonstrating a sentimental streak that might have surprised Leon Trotsky's minions, the bride kept a scrapbook filled with the vacation's menus, receipts, and pieces of memorabilia. Ever the dramatists, the duo posed for beach photographs in bathing suits, shaking hands as if they had first met. They made a stunning couple. Noting his curly black hair, hazel eyes, and rangy athletic frame, friends compared Nat to movie idol Jeff Chandler. "Dotty's" high cheekbones, golden skin, pitch-black hair, and lithe body, in turn, brought comparisons to Hollywood's Merle Oberon.

Upon returning home, the couple nestled into a series of West Bronx rooming houses. Yet marriage seemed to wear well. Nat's poem, "Love Song in the Bronx," touched on the possibilities:

> I held her hand and said to her,
> Though, dearest girl, you might prefer,
> A moonlit night in some bazaar
> In Cairo or in Zanzibar,
> Believe me, dear, it's better far,
> Being here, just where we are.
>
> High and far, remote, aloof,
> Our magic carpet is this roof.
> What is more exotic, dear,
> Than kissing in this atmosphere
>
> Antennas waving in the breeze,
> Midst drying socks and B.V.D.'s
> A beaming moon, a twinkling star,
> It's so nice just where you are.
>
> Haunting strains from taxi honks,
> It's a lovely evening in the Bronx.

43

Dorothy's verse, "To My Husband," conveyed an enviable intimacy:

When I come home to you tonight
My mind will be sweet peace
My hunger all appeased
And your hands shall reach for me.

Adopting the pen name, Dorothy Lee Harris, the new Mrs. Horowitz threw herself into fiction. A short story, "Blackout on Love," depicted romance on the Broadway burlesque circuit. Another, "Home with the Milkman," portrayed a humble and virtuous young woman whose innocent charms distract an upper-class suitor from the decadence of socialite New York. "They Have a World to Win," the novel she had launched in high school, centered on an autobiographical main character, a dreamer searching for the ultimate.

"Don't you see," Elsa declares, "I love children too well and that's why I couldn't bear to bring my child into a world of misery and war."

Like the author, the protagonist ignores ideological commitments to marry out of love. As promised, however, Dorothy did not abandon the movement. She even dragged her new husband to a few Trotskyist cell meetings. Despite the fact that he found the group's polemics bewildering and somewhat tedious, she dedicated a short play to him entitled "War."

"I hope the Revolution finally appears on our scene," Dorothy wrote, "so that we can both live a happy peaceful life—so that he won't have to die on a piece of barbed wire. And I hope he will help me fight."

The plot of "War" focused on a radical political group whose strategy meeting halts when the host's husband arrives home from work.

"He's sympathetic, but not ready to join with us," the activist explains.

When the crowd has gone, the wife asks for help in distributing leaflets denouncing militarism as "the bidding of the bosses." Fearing for her safety, he asks her not to attend the protest. Yet she insists she must act out of "loyalty to myself, to my ideals, and to my beliefs."

At that point, the radio broadcasts a declaration of war. Now the meeting will be even greater, exclaims the wife.

"It's our chance to tell the masses," she exults.

"They'll listen, they'll believe us, they'll come back to us, and we'll show them what to do. Won't we, my comrade husband?"

"Yes, my comrade turnip," he responds with a feeble smile.

Dorothy's fantasy could not anticipate the threat to radical antiwar solidarity that followed the August 1939 signing of a mutual defense pact between the Soviet Union and Nazi Germany and the outbreak of World War II. Trotskyists now claimed their predictions of Stalinist treachery had come true. In response, Dorothy composed a parody to "My Blue Heaven":

> Just Adolf and me
> And Molotoff makes three
> We're happy in my Red Heaven.

Meanwhile, both the American Socialist and Communist parties urged the United States to reject an alliance with "imperialist" Great Britain, a dilemma for American Jews and opponents of dictatorship who despised war but feared the rising menace of Hitlerism.

The Good Things

Given the deteriorating world situation, it is not surprising that Dorothy invested so much energy in the creative efforts of her husband. Even before the marriage, she had urged him to "work hard and brilliantly, please for me. There is so much within you, and I have tremendous confidence."

One result of her influence was the poem, "The New Culture," which Nat composed while in California. Dedicated "to that aesthetic soul, Bruno Mussolini, purveyor of fascist art," the verse has the dictator's aviator son describe the visual effects of dropping bombs on civilians:

> It's sport to pop a church's steeple
> And watch the funny running people
> I have to laugh the way they scurry
> I c'n get 'em however they hurry.

Once he returned from Los Angeles, "Nat Harris" dove into proletarian realism. The short story, "Punishment Without Crime," describes an eighteen-year-old Bronx hustler who parlays a week's wages into thirty dollars of crap-shooting winnings, only to be targeted by a stick-up on the way home for the Jewish Sabbath. The tale takes another twist when the would-be assailant collapses from a tubercular attack, inducing the protagonist to turn over his money in sympathy. After the gambler's Orthodox father brutally canes him for losing his pay, the ailing mugger shows up at the family apartment and reciprocates the young man's act of charity by returning the entire sum.

"Vengeance is Mine" offered another use of the ironic ending Nat admired in the short stories of O. Henry. Rendered in heavy dialect, the tale follows an Italian truck driver who runs down his best friend for sleeping with his new bride only to discover that the victim was about to commit suicide over the betrayal and had left a note asking for forgiveness. "Cozy Home," written sometime after the wedding, incorporated another element of irony. The story concerned a recently married but jobless renter who takes immense pride in the comfortable living quarters he and his wife have created only to realize he must call the storage company to remove the belongings before creditors repossess them.

The first year of the marriage also witnessed Nat's attempt to write socially conscious poetry. "Depression Days – October 7, 1938" provides a somber depiction of the downward journey of an evicted renter to the street, to the gutter, to the park, to the docks, and finally, to the river, where the superfluous man drowns himself.

"The tide brought him back," the final couplet reads.

"What shall we do with him?"

"Sixth Avenue, 1938" speculates about alleviating the hunger of the "sullen mass" treading along downtown streets but asks what would soothe the soul. Nat Harris's signature reflection of the times, however, was "The Buyer Said a Merry Xmas." The four-part verse drew on the author's experiences at Macy's to provide a series of heartfelt portraits of department store part-timers placed out on the street as the holiday retail season closes:

The buyer got up and said, "Thank you,
Each and every one of your for your cooperation."
. . . .
This was the last day
And that evening
All the people who had cooperated so splendidly
Were fired,
And their Christmas was not so merry.

Nat Harris sent an excerpt of "Vengeance is Mine" to the William Morris Agency, only to hear that the piece was "all well done and amusing, but not the type of material we can market for you." By this time, the aspiring writer had begun to mine other fields. Under the pseudonym, "Nathaniel Harris," he had written a Negro dialect verse, "Along De Way to Hebbin," that Charlie Kingsford set to music. Nat's long-held flair for Yiddish, Italian, Bronx, or Negro vernacular reflected a romantic fascination with the unpretentious qualities of character, piety, and family loyalty he saw in ordinary people. One of his models was George and Ira Gershwin's *Porgy and Bess* (1935), a folk opera staged by New York's Theater Guild that merged informal African American phrasing with the musical heritage of blues, jazz, and spirituals. *Green Pastures* (1936), a whimsical film with an all-black cast featuring "de Lawd" and a devoted band of angels and saints, provided additional inspiration.

After completing his musical training at Juilliard, Charlie had formed his own sheet music publishing house to adapt poetry for concert performances of voice and piano. One piece, "Command," found its way into the repertoire of Metropolitan Opera star Rise Stevens. Published in 1937 by the Carl Fischer house, "Along De Way to Hebbin" became the first of four Harris-Kingsford collaborations to make it into print, followed by "De Lawd's Dress-Suit," "Don' Ask Me, Lawd," and "Chicken Dinnah!" The last of the quartet was the most accessible. Composed as a bluesy jump tune, the song would attract a live radio performance by tenor Nelson Eddy in 1944.

"Thank the Lord for the good things!" the lyric begins. "There's nothing' better than the good things!"

The final stanza offered a hint of the whimsy infusing so many of Nady's creations:

> And thank you Lord, for the rain and crops,
> And if you're short of chicken, send pork chops!
> Oh, the Lord provides, the Lord, he brings
> The good things, the good things,
> Thank the Lord, thank the Lord, thank the Lord for the good things!

"Folk speech falls softly on my ears," Nathan would explain in later years—"picturesque distortions sometime cloth phrases and emotions with valuable down-to-earth simplicity."

Rather than mocking the exaggerated metaphors and occasional improprieties of Negro idiom, the unsophisticated humor, colorful modes of expression, and spiritual reverence of "Chicken Dinnah!" resonated with similar qualities the author cherished in Yiddish culture. In effect, "Nathaniel Harris"—the would-be black preacher—had described everything he loved about the Jewish people.

Photographs from the early years of the Horowitz marriage reveal an attractive couple freely cavorting with their "set" at Palisades Amusement Park or at holiday parties. Nat would always remember the hilarious send-up of Samson and Delilah friends Edie and Izzie performed at a New Year's Eve gathering. Yet the period following the honeymoon coincided with the most precipitous economic decline in U.S. history. As unemployment soared from seven to eleven million in 1938, Dorothy joined the army of desperate job seekers. She often recalled answering a Gimbels Department Store ad calling for female college graduates to serve as retail clerks in Foundations, the women's undergarment counter of the bargain basement.

"I'm sorry, dear," the interviewer told her.

"We're only hiring Vassar girls this week."

A Million Laughs

Just as prospects seemed bleak at year's end, Charlie Hertzig came up with two positions at Minsky's. The Miami Beach establishment had managed to sustain the traditional ingredients of burlesque with off-color stand-up comedy, comic skits, dance routines, and jazzy musical finales. Yet as the show's placards indicated, the strippers continued to be the main attraction:

> Sensational Strip-Tease
> GORGEOUS GIRLS
> A MILLION LAUGHS
> CAST OF 70
>
> Don't Dare return North
> Without first seeing
> The Only and Original
>   MINSKY'S
> Known The World Over

Once the newlyweds returned to the land of everlasting sun and smiles, where the Levines ran a South Beach café called "Pigs at Besses," Nat finally had steady work. Using Harris as his handle once again, he served as "Head Supervisor of Distribution"—the "barker" who beckoned customers into the hall. Dorothy's credentials as a college graduate qualified her for a slot as box-office cashier. She kept a detailed scrapbook of material for potential writing projects, including the "Rundown"—the order of the revue's sketches—and "The Broken Record"—the in-house gossip sheet. Dorothy also recorded the list of literary and political authors she and Nat read, including André Malraux, Ernest Hemingway, Pearl Buck, John Dos Passos, Diego Rivera, Sherwood Anderson, Willa Cather, Madame Curie, and Russian novelist Mikhail Aleksandrovich Sholokhov.

In May 1939, Hertzig transferred the couple to the New York World's Fair at Flushing Meadows, Queens, where his son, Manny, was co-producer of the N. T. G. Congress of Beauty. Erected around the theme of "The World of Tomorrow," the Fair placed the "trylon," a triangular needle skyscraper, and the adjoining "Perisphere," a huge domed structure housing a model city, at its center. Other attractions included Futurama—designer Norman Bel Geddes's prototype of a revolutionary nationwide road system—the first 3-D motion picture, and the inaugural display of television—dramatized by live coverage of the opening ceremony and daily telecasts from the RCA pavilion.

"The Congress of Sixty Beauties of the World" sat in the Midway amusement section along an artificial lake near the southern gate subway stop. Its neighbors included the Bel Geddes Dance Show, Billy Rose's Aquacade, and the Savoy Theater, where legendary African American tap dancer "Bojangles" Robinson performed. For forty cents, the *New York Times* reported, spectators at the Congress could walk around an unobstructed Garden of Eden inhabited by scores of "the World's Fairest" women, "clad mostly in chiffon leaves," and take photographs as the beauties played games, rode ponies, and took sun baths. Another twenty-five cents permitted patrons to attend "a four-unit stage show including a fan dance to end all fan dances."

Once again, Dorothy's college degree led to a position in the box office. The photo on her employee identification card, which she retained among family mementos, reveals a clear-eyed and alert young woman with a stylishly tilted beret atop her head. Nat wound up as a "candy butcher"—the iced drink dispenser and program peddler. One evening the souvenir pitchman failed to show and Harris had to appear before 1600 people under the jammed tent.

"The man and the lady in the glass cage!" he barked, "a prize in each and every package, ladies and gentlemen."

Family Planning

The luxury of dual incomes lasted until August 1939 when an indecency rap against one of the "fan dancers" and exorbitant rental fees and other costs forced the Congress of Beauty to fold two months before the Fair itself closed. By then, Nathan and Dorothy had set up housekeeping in a West Bronx studio apartment on Davidson Avenue. Sometime that year, Dorothy clipped a newspaper ad for *The Great Man Votes*, a film starring John Barrymore with a director's credit to Garson Kanin. Arriving in Hollywood in 1937 and finding a place in movie mogul Sam Goldwyn's production staff, Gar had become one of the industry's young successes. The Barrymore film was his fourth directorial effort. Meanwhile, Mike Kanin had joined his brother in movie land and signed on with RKO as a screenwriter.

Amid the good fortune of old friends, Nat searched for work. An interview with the Cashman Diaper Service seemed to do the trick when the neatly furnished Davidson Avenue apartment and the quiet intelligence and demeanor of the applicant's college-educated wife left a favorable impression with the company representative. For twenty-five dollars a week, Nat now had a job driving a delivery truck in the affluent and predominantly Gentile suburbs of Westchester County, just north of the Bronx. One day he slipped on an icy sidewalk, nearly breaking his arm. On another occasion, the ghosts of anti-Semitism appeared to resurface when a traffic cop pulled him over and asked for his driver's license.

"Well, Na-than Hor-o-witz," the officer responded with a condescending deliberateness the driver interpreted as a mockery of his Jewish-sounding name.

Elated, nevertheless, to be bringing home a steady paycheck, Nat agreed to move into roomier quarters. The result was a second-story studio apartment at 1495 Popham Avenue, a well-maintained rent control building in the University Heights district of the West Bronx. The six-floor Townsend Arms sat on the crest of a hill within a stone's throw of a Roman Catholic convent at the end of the street. The distinguished brick-faced edifice featured a courtyard entrance with well-kept shrubs and a tiled, mansard roof. Built in the 1920s, it had originally boasted a doorman and a jitney serving the Jerome Avenue Elevated. Even as late as 1940, the large and efficiently running elevator remained the envy of the block.

In November, shortly after a lottery initiated the first peacetime military draft in U.S. history, Dorothy missed her period. As she experienced severe morning sickness over the next several weeks, she decided to winter in Miami with her parents, who now ran a boarding house on S.W. 2nd Street off Flagler Avenue. Separated once again, Dorothy sent her husband daily letters.

"Don't work too hard, honey, to hell with the diapers," she admonished in her first note.

"So, we'll sleep in a palm tree and eat coconuts."

Another confessed "a hot dream about you last night, you bad boy."

"Whenever I think of you baby, I think of you in these surroundings, as—on our honeymoon, or when we worked at Minsky's. I never try to picture you in the city's clutches."

A few days later, Dorothy boasted that she had prepared a Jewish meal of *gefilte* fish, *knadlech* soup, breast of beef, *potato latkes*, green peas, and iced tea, all Nat's favorites.

"I want to cook for you," she promised in a subsequent letter:

> I want to walk and talk with you. I want to hear you take showers, wash your teeth, drop your shoes off. I want to sleep with you, thrill you to death, I want to sit next to you in a movie, I want to hear your troubles, I want to laugh with you, I want to kiss you, I want to say "bring me a glass of water, honey,"—I want to say "Bring me the Kleenex, it's dark—I can't find it come back to bed, honey, and hold me tight."

"I'm very hot for you," Dorothy exclaimed on another occasion.

"I want to be a wild bad girl with you."

"I'm your wife, the mother of your child, the light of your life, the essence of your soul, the one and only woman in your sex life."

Beyond the heated confessions of a young woman in the early stages of pregnancy, Dorothy's correspondence conveyed a profound ambivalence about the prospects awaiting a newborn child. As a socialist and pacifist, she struggled, like Elsa in "They Have a World to Win," about bringing an infant into a world at war, even if the threats of fascism and Nazism seemed to require it. Three days before her first letter in early January 1941, President Franklin D. Roosevelt delivered a fireside chat declaring the United States to be the arsenal of democracy in the confrontation with Axis aggression.

"Did you listen to Roosevelt's speech?" her note asked.

"I try not to think of the impending war. Our baby is going to be a welcomed child. I don't even want to feel regretful about bringing a new life on this world."

Nevertheless, Dorothy found it increasingly difficult to sort out her feelings about the struggle against the Nazis. Arguing with her father, she found herself so emotionally overwrought she took sick and concluded she would not be able to talk politics for a while. This only added to Dorothy's sense of guilt. Marveling at the way her mother pampered her, she apologized for being an escapist and a coward.

"I'm blotting out the truth, but I won't allow myself to think," she reported.

"For 2 months I'll pretend people are as happy as I am—all over the world."

Such delusions, however, were difficult to sustain.

"You can imagine the pangs of conscience I get," Dorothy explained, "when I lie on the beach and look up at the planes spilling harmless advertising instead of bombs."

Then she consoled herself. "I was sick," she reasoned, "I'm going to have a baby, I worked a little in my life, I even worked for Socialism a little while, there will be even greater struggles in the future."

"I feel sorry for the shackled in Europe, Asia, Africa, America," she continued, yet "what can I do? We are all helpless without organization and leadership."

Despite such regrets, Dorothy relished the prospect of the life inside her."

"Everything is so miraculous," she wrote, "I'm almost beginning to believe in a God."

"Who could have designed the body with such logical, minute, wonderful details?"

Once again, however, she countered with the thought that "you must think me shallow and cruel to be able to be so happy and full of life—in these horrible times."

At the end of January, Dorothy joked that she had weighed herself on a penny scale that also told fortunes and learned she would have two boys. On February 22nd, the eve of their third anniversary, the couple reunited in the Bronx. Looking to an August delivery, Dorothy hoped to channel utopian political aspirations into a materially secure and loving family sustained by artistic creativity, cultural activism, and enlightened social conscience. Nat, in turn, sought to honor a lifelong passion for self-expression while acceding to the irrevocable responsibilities of parenthood and a family.

Davidovitch

Not long after Dorothy's return, the couple relocated across the hall to a three-room spread. Although the living room and kitchen of Apartment 2-F looked out to a courtyard, the spacious bedroom faced west to the Harlem River and Upper Manhattan's Washington Heights. Looking past the limbs of the ancient elms in the vacant lots below, one could follow the trains on the New York Central Railroad tracks and the barges and tugboats on the river beyond them. Across the water, the domed Yeshiva University and nearby George Washington High School appeared on a bluff amid a row of handsome apartment buildings.

Seeking to distinguish themselves from the crowd, Nat and Dorothy furnished the new apartment in rustic Early American décor. Their carved white oak bedroom set included matching twin beds, a night table, and two dressers. A color print of a Mary Cassatt painting of a mother and child, clipped from a magazine and subsequently framed, hung on the wall. The rest of the layout featured an assortment of maple furniture that included a cobbler's bench coffee table, a quaint standing lamp with a built-in bookshelf, and a rocker. Miniature prints of Michelangelo's *David*, Edgar Degas's ballet dancers, and other works added to the ambiance. A tall maple bookshelf contained Dorothy's collection of Marxian texts and economy editions of the complete works of Charles Dickens and Samuel Clemens.

Early in the year, Nat had proposed that if the baby were a boy, he would like to call him David Alan in honor of his maternal grandfather, *Avrom Duvid*.

"*David is for Davidovitch!*" an elated Dorothy responded, a reference to *Lev Davidovitch Bronstein*, the given name of Leon Trotsky, murdered months earlier by a Stalinist agent in Mexico. On Father's Day, the prospective mother composed a greeting from the baby:

> Though I know that you are avid
> For a regal son named David,
> Please don't bear *me* any malice
> If my mummy bears an Alice.
>
> Daddy, dear, I love you now
> For all those things you'll teach me how:
> To throw a ball, to tell the time,
> To ride a bike, to write some rhyme,
> To love the rain, to climb a tree,
> To hum a tune, to paint the sea.
>
> And later maybe the Bronx Park Zoo
> (If that won't be too much for you)
> The Macy Parade, a Disney reel
> Although you might prefer "Camille."
>
> But all these treats must wait for me
> Until I smile and hear and see.
> In fact, dear dad, I'm quite forlorn
> It's so lonely until one's born.
> But don't be nervous, don't you fret,
> I'll make you a father yet!

By the time Dorothy went into labor that summer, a seasonal heat wave had dissipated. Nevertheless, she experienced a prolonged delivery before a baby boy finally emerged on Sunday afternoon, August 17th.

The couple sent out cards announcing "the Inaugural Address of David Alan Horowitz."

Dorothy's meticulous memory book described a sturdy infant with a tiny dimple on the left cheek, long sideburns, and small puffy eyes. One minute after birth, she watched her son place his thumb in his mouth and widen his pupils. Circumcised at home the next month, David Alan yelped and quickly returned to his milk bottle. Dutiful entries in the baby book noted the first time he ingested cod liver oil and orange juice, handled a rattle, grasped at his bottle, recognized his parents, cut his first teeth, crawled, crept, stood up, climbed, ate in his high chair, walked, and uttered initial syllables. At first, Dorothy despaired over her clumsiness in changing diapers but learned to relax her charge with Beethoven symphonies before five o'clock baths and evening feedings.

On December 8, 1941, the memory book noted that David Alan had ingested his first vegetables—carrots. A parenthesis recorded the fact that the United States had declared war on Japan the day after Pearl Harbor.

Three days before the boy's delivery, President Roosevelt and British Prime Minister Winston Churchill had signed the Atlantic Charter and committed themselves to a world free of fascism. The day after David took his first breath, Roosevelt approved an eighteen-month extension of the military draft. Sanctioned by a single vote majority in the House of Representatives, the law exempted men employed in essential industries. This may have influenced Nat to join Dorothy's high school beau, Rube Cheroff, at Diehl's, an electrical components defense plant near Elizabeth, New Jersey. The punch press that Nat operated registered seven thousand strokes an hour. Rising at 4 a.m., he spent nearly five hours a day commuting to and from work by subway and a series of bus connections.

Little David celebrated his first birthday in the cocktail lounge of the Broadway Casino. Nattily attired in a long-sleeved white shirt with an arrow collar and a plaid tie in his Taylor-Tot, the toddler kept rhythm to the jukebox while the grown-ups shared cake, cookies, scotch, and rye. Birthday gifts included musical blocks and a fifty-dollar war bond. Christmas brought a Snow White toy chest, a Victory Bond, and a recording of Prokofiev's "Peter and the Wolf."

Dorothy's meticulously detailed memory book attributed the boy's dark complexion and eyes to his mother, his body proportions and facial contours to his father, and his "sunny" disposition to himself.

A poem celebrated his second birthday:

> Can it be that you're just two?
> Just two years, my little son?
> (How I try to fathom
> The miracle you are!)
> Can it be two years ago,
> For surely I was born again!
> There comes a Joy Unknown,
> In the agony of Birth.
> "Dialectics," we should have named you.
> Oh, how glad I am we called you David.

David A. Horowitz

VJ Kid

David's first meeting with Uncle Milt occurred in Brooklyn. Serving as vice-president of a predominantly Jewish state public employees union, Milt's Trotskyist sympathies and anti-Soviet views had offended the organization's powerful Communist bloc. Retreating to his parents' boarding house in Florida, he agonized, as did his sister, over reconciling a profound distrust of war with an abiding hatred of Nazism.

"How was Hitler to be stopped?" he remembered thinking. "Was my Jewishness interfering with my revolutionary resolve?"

Sometime after Pearl Harbor, Milt resolved the dilemma by enlisting in the Army.

"Maybe the United States was just involved in another imperialist war," he later recalled, "I was going to fight Hitler and Mussolini."

Stationed in Oakland, California, Milt encouraged fellow soldiers to call him by his former nickname, Mickey, the handle his nephew learned to address him by as the newly striped sergeant returned on furlough in September 1943. "Brownie" camera photographs of the visit show Uncle Mickey cavorting with David on the cement veranda behind the Popham Avenue building, where the two-year-old learned to mimic Army phrases like "tell-me-something" and "that's the ticket!"

The following summer, Nathan and Dorothy rented a bungalow with Rube Cheroff and his wife Rose at Lake Hopatcong in western New Jersey. Snapshots of the period reveal a relaxed, pipe-smoking Nat in a sailor's cap and tight swim trunks while Dorothy appears in a striking black bathing suit edged with white frills. Seemingly protected from the ravages of the war, the family of three bonded in a cocoon of security and love. In place of bedtime readings, Nat spun a series of invented stories about "the three little boys," a trio entitled to highly anticipated adventures to the circus, parades, and other treats when they had been good. On other occasions, father, mother, and son bonded by holding hands and dancing in a circle singing "dee-dee-dee."

Nat and Dorothy exposed their son to a variety of music. Listening to records or the radio for hours, David soon learned to sway to the rhythm of each piece in his miniature rocking chair or on the large, maple rocker alongside it. Favorite performers included Bing Crosby, Frank Sinatra, Al Jolson, Burl Ives ("Jimmy Crack Corn"), and the Andrew Sisters. Dorothy even claimed he could tap-dance and sing along to Jimmy Cagney's

"Yankee Doodle Dandy" while adding original rhymes to his own rhythms. The boy's proud parents also reported that he enjoyed classical pieces such as "Peter and the Wolf," Dvorak's "New World Symphony," and the works of Tchaikovsky.

Dorothy and David spent a good deal of time with neighbors and their children in "the backyard," the elevated rear terrace of the Townsend Arms. The space offered a perfect setting for a hopscotch game called "Potsie" and tricycle riding. Because wartime rationing eliminated the production of bikes, Dorothy had to drag her son on a long trek across the Harlem River to a second-hand moving and storage outfit in Washington Heights to secure one for six dollars. The price included the pedal blocks required by David's short legs. At first, he would only pedal backwards. Yet once mastering the art of cycling, David joined his pals in racing from one end of the terrace to the other. He even learned to frighten bystanders on the front sidewalk by bringing the bike to a screeching stop at the edge of the curb without crossing into the forbidden street.

Family outings extended to the Miramar swimming pool and to the Bronx Zoo, where Nat photographed his son astride a llama. Brief neighborhood excursions were far more frequent. Teddy, Bernie, and their daughters Dale and Isabel resided on the first floor of an art deco, white-brick apartment building about three blocks north on Popham Avenue. The four-room unit boasted a sunken living room and two bathrooms, tokens of unheard luxury, and Sandy, the family cocker spaniel. Becky and Barnett shared a three-room apartment two blocks from Teddy in an old structure with a tiny, gated elevator that creaked ominously. In the opposite direction, down the hill to Plympton Avenue, Sam Harris and his crew rented a semi-attached layout that boasted an upright piano in the front parlor. On the way home, Nat always stopped to let his son see the triangular lot he called "the farm," where the owner grew tomatoes, lettuce, and beans.

In the early morning hours of September 2, 1945—VJ (Victory over Japan) Day marking the official end of World War II—the intimate family circle expanded. At 1:45 in the morning, babysitter Bess Levine awakened her grandson to tell him he had a baby brother, Michael Gene, whose middle name honored the memory of his great-grandmother, Geneshe, as well as Levine idol, Socialist Eugene Debs.

A month after the circumcision, the five-week-old infant traveled in a basket to Pennsylvania Station, where the family caught the train for Miami. With Nat finally free of the defense plant and the apartment subleased to a friend, the couple planned a temporary stay at the Levine boarding house while Nat considered a venture in the retail grocery business with Mickey, now released from the Army.

Stationed in Hawaii as the war ended, Mickey had helped to found the pioneering chapter of the liberal American Veterans Committee (AVC). The organization's slogan, "Citizens First, Veterans Second," embodied a New Deal, racially inclusive, and internationalist agenda that contrasted with the conservative and whites-only American Legion. While Mickey weighed a future in retail, hotel management, or Florida politics, he had time to introduce his four-year-old nephew to movie treats that included *Dumbo*, *Song of the South*, and *The Harvey Girls*.

Back in the Bronx

Over the course of her courtship and marriage, Dorothy continually had warned Nat about falling under the influence of her parents.

"Let's keep our little independence and little security and tiny peace of mind," she had written early in 1941.

Consequently, it may not have come as a complete disappointment to her when five months after the family's arrival in Florida, Teddy Mass called from New York. Barnett's vascular ailments and depression had taken a terrible turn, requiring his placement in a convalescent home. Teddy begged her brother to return to the Bronx.

Suddenly, all Miami plans were in limbo and Nat and Dorothy were apart once more. Desperate for work, Nat followed up when brother Sam recommended him to his employer—the sales department of the West Disinfecting Company, a Long Island City manufacturer of industrial cleansers and sanitary products.

"The world is waiting for you, my boy," the branch manager told the new man on his first day in March 1946.

The position offered a fifty-dollar a week guarantee, a figure the company subtracted from any commissions above that sum. Using Sam's last name out of simple convenience, "Nat Harris" started from scratch, "knocking on doors" as he later described it, in a frenzied search for clients. Yet he found himself in a growing field in a postwar economic boom and prided himself in never letting commissions lag behind salary. Within six weeks, the novice sales representative had broken all company records and was bringing in a hundred dollars of receipts a day. He quickly would become the top revenue producer in a firm with fifty nationwide branches. Meanwhile, as a dutiful son, he visited the ailing Barnett weekend afternoons and at the close of most workdays.

By Labor Day, the Horowitz family had reclaimed the Bronx apartment. Life in the neighborhood hardly varied from what Nat and Dorothy had experienced as children. Two blocks down the hill, University Avenue featured Eddie's corner candy store and Phil Campanella's barbershop, where Nat ruled out any use of hair tonic. Other amenities included the Hebrew National deli, a kosher supermarket, and a "commission" bakery where Orthodox immigrants sold fresh rye bread, loaves of *challah*, Kaiser rolls, and a variety of bagels, jellyrolls, Danish pastry, and "black and white" chocolate-vanilla sweet cakes. Despite concerns about frugality, Nat insisted that Dorothy never stint on the quality of food, particularly at the kosher butcher shop. His instructions also included an absolute prohibition of starch on his shirts at the Chinese laundry.

On Sundays, Nat and David walked down to the trolley line for the ride to a park by Yankee Stadium, where the perennial handball player returned to the athletic routines of youth and David explored beneath the nearby highway ramps. At home, the radio served as a mainstay of evening entertainment. While Nat and Dorothy permitted David to listen to the Lone Ranger, they preferred the comedy routines of Fred Allen, Jack Benny, and (George) Burns and (Gracie) Allen. Household popular music favorites included Bing Crosby's "Swinging on a Star" with its emphasis on the virtues of schooling, Judy Garland's "Trolley Song," and Dinah Shore's "Blues in the Night."

When inspired, David serenaded Michael in his crib with vocal renditions of "I'm Looking over a Fear Leaf Clover" or *Song of the South*'s "Zip-a Dee-Doo-Dah." Yet the protected routines of child life came to an abrupt end in September 1946 when Nat escorted the five-year-old to P. S. 104 for the start of kindergarten. Panicked at the prospect of submitting to the authority of strangers, David kicked the rotund Irish American female principal in the behind before resigning himself to his fate.

When the school year ended the following June, Nat and Dorothy sought relief from the city's sweltering heat by renting a bungalow in Babylon on Long Island's south shore, close enough to Manhattan to enable Nat to commute by Long Island Railroad. David enjoyed taking extended walks with his father down the area's rustic country lanes, where, on one occasion, they bonded over the discovery of a rusted-out wrench. Yet the seedy clapboard rental reignited Dorothy's memories of Lake Huntington, particularly when the roof leaked over Mikey's crib and David came down with impetigo—a contagious skin infection likely contracted in the bacteria-laden local swimming pond.

Back in the Bronx, Nat was pleased that David had joined the Spalding rubber ball games of stickball, punch ball, "off-the-curb," box ball, and "captain"—a pavement version of handball—that he had engaged in as a boy. When a blizzard dumped twenty-six-inches of snow in December, 1947, moreover, the backyard terrace of the building provided the perfect setting for ice forts and snowball battles. By then, David had a Flexible Flyer sled—perfect for a "belly whop" on the uninterrupted stretch of sidewalk along the convent wall leading down 174th Street to University Avenue.

Nat particularly enjoyed the prospect of David and his pals roaming the backyard lots, "riding the trails," digging out infantry "foxholes," excavating stubborn boulders, and playing cowboys and Indians. He even composed a poem about the colorful crew:

> Up from the coal mines black with grime,
> Streaked with dust and dirt and lime,
> Caked with the mud of perspiring earth,
> Grinning with boisterous and cackling mirth,
> Striding and running with agile gait –
> Up from the mines! The triumvirate!
> the lords and masters of all about.

Imperfect

By the time Nat committed the verse to paper, however, his rambunctious son was sporting eyeglasses. A note from David's first grade teacher described his difficulty in reading the blackboard. Neither parent had a history of impaired vision. Yet a visit to the optometrist revealed that their son was myopic and in need of thick corrective lenses. When David exclaimed how "light" everything was when he tried on the new spectacles, Nat and Dorothy felt twinges of guilt over the failure to take notice of the impairment. Besides, the prospect of their six-year-old with cumbersome glasses on his nose was a blow to expectations of a perfect family.

David seemed cheerful about the adjustment but it soon became clear his self-confidence had taken a hit. Dorothy, in fact, had to plead with the mother of a neighboring boy to rescue her bespectacled son from repeated bullying.

For his part, Nat always urged David to remove his glasses when posing for family snapshots.

4

MOVING ON UP

Like the eastern European *shtetl*, the Townsend Arms was a village unto itself. When the janitor was slow to stoke up the furnace on cold days, impatient tenants banged insistently on the steam radiators. On late-afternoons or weekends, residents could hear the cry of "I cash clothes" (the "I" came out as "Hi") from a full-bearded street peddler soliciting resale garments from the pavement below. Other times, an unkempt old man in a bedraggled overcoat would offer a melancholy violin serenade from the courtyard and collect the coins tossed below.

Living for the City

Most of the building's neighbors were comforting figures in a well-defined and predictable world. On the ground floor, Ida and Benny Friedman squeezed crowds of children into their tiny living room to watch 5 p.m. screenings of Howdy Doody on a ten-inch Admiral TV. Meanwhile, appliance repairer Morris Levin cracked off-color jokes as he chewed on a half-lit cigar and roamed the halls in greasy overalls. In contrast, Mr. Epstein, a concert violinist, brought civility and high culture to the environment, as did the Marks family, refugees from Nazi Germany whose elder daughter practiced opera solos in the hallways.

There were few secrets at 1495, particularly when a chorus of homemakers gathered on bridge chairs along the front pavement in good weather. If a breadwinner lost a job, everyone would soon know it. When a blonde Gentile spouse who sported high-heels and tailored clothes began knitting a sweater for another child, the gossipers whispered that her husband "doesn't leave her alone." The comely librarian on the third floor who had lost her husband in the war also elicited sympathy. Then there was Mrs. Lieberman, one of David's former babysitters, who sometimes paced the corridors late at night with a ragged white wool shawl over her shoulders, emitting chilling wails. Rumor held she was calling a fallen son from the Pacific. Invariably, Dorothy would ask Nat to calm the poor soul down and coax her back to her apartment.

None of these tenants elicited as much attention as the most unpleasant and disreputable family in the building. Married to a loud peroxide blonde, the head of the clan, a coarse and heavy-set kosher butcher, drove a flashy Buick sedan. One winter the couple departed for Miami with their two sons. It turned out the butcher had substituted *trafe* for the ritualistically blessed, blood-drained, and more expensive kosher meat required by Orthodox dietary laws. Once the clan returned, their older son Stanley took to tossing chunks of ice off the roof, mounting BB gun assaults on passers-by, and setting fire to the lots, dumbwaiters, and elevator shafts.

For the summer of 1948, Nat and Dorothy found a brick rental on Long Island at Long Beach, only blocks from the Atlantic Ocean. They were thrilled that Mike Kanin and his wife Fay planned to spend the season nearby while their new Broadway play went into rehearsal. Both Kanin brothers had prospered since their arrival in Hollywood.

63

David A. Horowitz

After directing Cary Grant and Irene Dunne in *My Favorite Wife* (1940) and filming two other hits, Gar had worked on wartime government documentaries before returning to Broadway, where he served as the author and director of the comic classic *Born Yesterday* (1946). For his part, Mike had shared a screenwriting Academy Award for *Woman of the Year* (1942), the first motion picture to co-star movie icons Spencer Tracy and Katharine Hepburn.

With the inspiration provided by the Kanins, Nat and Dorothy began writing a three-act psychological drama in the fall of 1948. Spending late evenings at the kitchen table, they nevertheless found it necessary to deal with three-year-old Mikey. When her youngest had turned two, the age at which specialists called for replacing baby bottles, Dorothy celebrated with a humorous ditty:

> At 14 months, I can use a BRIBE.
> At 15 months, a DIATRIBE
> At a year and a half, I can whack your REAR,
>   perhaps instill a harmless FEAR.
> . . . .
> You're two years old! At last! Enough's been SAID –
> Hurrah! I can break the bottle over your head!

After a surgeon removed Mikey's tonsils, Dorothy came up with another poem:

> My name is Mike,
> A cute little tyke,
> To become remotely Freudian,
> I was "par-adenoidian."
> So my doc kept a-fillin'
> My rear with penna-cillin.
> And now there's a void
> Where once was lymphoid.

Not long after Mikey's procedure, however, he began to complain of difficulties in swallowing and refused to eat solid foods. As Dorothy anguished over failing in her most fundamental duty, her son lost weight, weakened, and seemed to lose interest in life. At wit's end, she consulted a woman psychiatrist recommended by the Jewish Board of Guardians, who speculated that the crisis might have had roots in the infection preceding the tonsillectomy. In the end, the therapist devised a soft-food diet with enough nutrition to take the emotional edge off the test of wills between mother and son. Dorothy emerged from the experience with a new respect for psychology but for years, Mikey's meals mainly consisted of grape jelly sandwiches on white bread minus the crusts.

Culture

When the summer of 1949 brought a nationwide polio scare, health officials urged parents to keep children out of public swimming facilities. Deciding to stay home, Nat and Dorothy enrolled both boys at Castle Hill Day Camp in the East Bronx near the handball courts Nady had used as a young man. Unused to strange foods, Mikey lasted only a day but his brother overcame his distaste for regimentation, the camp's limited recreational agenda, and the long daily bus rides to stick it out

Since early childhood, David had absorbed a taste for bluesy popular tunes such as "Chattanooga Choo-Choo" and "The Atchison, Topeka, and the Santa Fe." When the Levines had returned to New York in 1947 to open the Whitehall—a bar and catering establishment in one of Charlie Hertzig's hotels on Upper Broadway—visits to the lounge afforded the opportunity to experience the bubbling colors and bass frequencies of the jukebox's intoxicating numbers.

As an attractive young woman counselor sang a languid ballad backed by the sparsely placed chords of a piano accompanist during Castle Hill's season-ending amateur show, David fixated on the stage. Having tickled the ivories of the front parlor upright at Uncle Sam's house and been treated to the children's record of "Rusty and His Piano," he soon announced that he was ready for Charlie Kingsford to give him piano lessons. Nat replied he would be happy to pay for the instruction and even purchase an upright piano, but his son had to take the responsibility seriously and practice every day.

The two then struck a deal: if his parents refrained from constant reminders about the need to prepare his lessons, David would commit to an hour a day of practice.

Following the agreement, Nat followed Charlie's advice that only pre-World War II pianos maintained their tuning and purchased a studio upright for $250, equal to two weeks of West commissions. To fulfill his part of the arrangement, David now placed an alarm clock on top of the instrument to monitor promised practice time.

Over the next year-and-a-half, Nat devoted Saturday mornings to escorting his older son by bus and subway to Charlie's West 57th Street studio—a fourth floor tenement "walk-up" above the famed Russian Tea Room, literally a door from Carnegie Hall. Adhering to Charlie's insistence on maintaining the sanctity of the student-teacher relationship, Nat retreated to the nearby Horn and Hardart Cafeteria (the "Automat") for Danish pastry and coffee for the hour. At that, Charlie confided to his former collaborator that David lacked a rudimentary sense of rhythm but since he wanted to take lessons, he would see what he could do. Meanwhile, Dorothy took the boys on weekly treks to the small public library a mile from Popham Avenue where David devoured children's biographies of the great classical composers.

Not long after the piano assumed a place in the Horowitz living room, a twelve-inch-screen Magnavox television joined it. The set came in an attractive French provincial cabinet with a "distressed" fruitwood finish. To facilitate access to classical music, it featured a 33-rpm long-playing automatic "high-fidelity" record changer and an AM-FM radio. The first recording Dorothy purchased was *Faust*, her favorite opera, soon supplemented by a variety of classical collections. Yet when the Hi-Fi wires kept smoking and the TV needed constant repair, she would joke that the cabinet was not its only "distressed" feature.

Anxious to use television for cultural uplift, Nat and Dorothy encouraged the boys to watch educational programs such as *Mr. I-Magination*—"the Man with the Magic Reputation!" On Sunday afternoons, the entire family gathered for the high-minded arts cavalcade, Omnibus, hosted by Britain's distinguished Alistair Cooke. As aspiring playwrights, moreover, the couple devoured the live drama of early Fifties series such as *Philco TV Playhouse* and *Kraft Television Theater* and even invited David to join in viewing and discussing these programs.

At the same time, lighter fare had its day. Nat loved ethnic comedians such as Milton Berle, Edgar Bergen, Victor Borge, and especially, Sam Levenson, the leading chronicler of working-class Jewish family life. Another favorite was the Saturday evening *Show of Shows*, a ninety-minute variety mix that highlighted the manic improvisations and parodies of Sid Caesar, Carl Reiner, Howard Morris, and Imogene Coca. TV comic stars like Jack Benny, Fred Allen, Ed Wynn, George Jessel, Jimmy Durante, and Eddie Cantor brought back memories of vaudeville and radio, although Dorothy anguished at the handkerchief-wielding Sophie Tucker, whose routines already seemed dated when she had experienced them as a Minsky's cashier in Miami.

"Isn't she dead, yet?" Dotty cried at each appearance of "the last of the red hot mamas."

Getting On

With the polio scare in abeyance, the family spent the summer of 1950 at Strolowitz's Bungalow Colony in the Catskills. By the Fifties, nearly two thousand of these settlements dotted the region. On weekends, Nat made the two-hundred-mile round-trip commute with Bernie Mass, whose family rented a place in the same complex. The two-room Horowitz bungalow, set on concrete pillars, was on the less expensive side of the enclave a distance from the private spring-fed lake. Yet the unit had a small porch Mikey rarely left that accommodated Nat's hammock. Beyond that, Strolie's boasted a softball field, handball court, small grocery, and newly built "casino" social hall. Nat took particular interest in the set of wild blueberry bushes that bordered the property, prompting him to organize family outings to collect "free" fruit in strung kitchen pots for the sour cream treats he loved and for additions to the boys' cold breakfast cereal.

Early in the season, Nat lost his father. He occasionally had brought the boys on weekend visits to the East Bronx's "Hebrew Home for Incurables," where Barnett had been consigned since 1948. There, the bald-headed and stoic former presser lay passively amid the crowded ward's odors of urine and disinfectant. His death certificate listed "general debilitation" as the cause of his demise, arguably the plight of an Old World figure unable to acclimate to America's hard tenor of life. Insisting on preserving the boys' summer respite from the city, Nat did not have the family attend the funeral. Once returning to the mountains for weekends, however, he followed Jewish custom by not shaving for a month and attending synagogue services twice a day to recite the mourner's *kaddish* in memory of the dead.

Just as the eleven-month period of Jewish bereavement ended the following spring, Nat purchased a $2,000 dark cherry red, two-door, manual transmission 1951 Studebaker Champion with a chrome airplane ornament on the hood. He now drove David through Central Park to Saturday morning piano lessons. Beyond that, the Studebaker enabled excursions to Van Cortland Park, Rye Beach, and Long Beach, as well as to President Roosevelt's Hyde Park estate up the Hudson. The family even spent a Thanksgiving or two with Eva and Nathan Herman in New Bedford. More immediately, ownership of a vehicle permitted a bungalow rental at Strolie's for the Memorial Day holiday. When it rained the entire time, Dorothy continually assured everyone it was "getting lighter." Born out of a maternal desire to maintain family morale, the mantra soon joined references to David's endless day camp bus rides as a comic point of reference.

On June 30th, normally the last day of school, Nat cleared the Studebaker trunk of its samples of West cleansers for the trip to the mountains. The leading challenge for the lightly powered Studebaker was the stop-and-go traffic on the Wurtsboro hill on two-lane Route 17, where the single signal light in the small town could tie up vehicles for hours. Rumor had it that anti-Semitic locals had timed the light to impede access to the Jewish resorts. Meanwhile, Nat took enormous pride in providing the chance for his boys to play safely on green grass in mountain air far from hot city pavements. He also promoted the manly virtues of athletic prowess. Softball performed an important role in this regard. Almost every snapshot of his sons at Strolie's involved staged hitting, fielding, or base slides, although Mikey had little interest in sports and simply put up a front for the camera.

Greener Pastures

The most significant consequence of owning a car involved the possibility of a move to the suburbs. For years, Nat and Dorothy had gone through a nightly ritual of transferring the boys from the twin beds of the apartment's sole bedroom to a dual living room trundle bed. In the cramped quarters of Apartment 2-F, the foyer also doubled as a playroom. Like many Americans who experienced the Great Depression and the war, the couple had dreamed of owning a house. Nat even celebrated the attractions of Suburbia with a parody.

"Oh, give me a home," went the verse, "where the fixtures are chrome...where sometime is heard, the sweet song of a bird":

Home – home for a change –
Where the roof and the pipes do not leak,
Where sometime is seen,
Some grass growing green
On our lawns ev'ry day in the week.

Another consideration involved the neighborhood. During President Roosevelt's re-election campaign in 1944, Dorothy had beaten out budding playwright Arthur Miller in a competition for a radio script on public housing sponsored by the Political Action Committee of labor's Congress of Industrial Organizations (CIO). The lead character of *Mrs. Blight Goes Abnormal* realizes the only way to cure her obsession over poor housing and homelessness is to replace the slums. Four year later, Dorothy's social conscience returned to haunt her when the New York City Planning Commission approved a public housing complex at the site of the old convent at the end of Popham Avenue. Despite objections that the neighborhood already was densely populated and lacked adequate recreational facilities and parking space, planners based their decision on the need for affordable housing for returning veterans and low-income families.

Dorothy considered herself a racial progressive. When an allergy to detergents prompted her to solicit help in cleaning the apartment, Agnes, the elderly West Indian woman who showed up each week, became a member of the family's inner circle. During an elevated subway ride through Harlem, Nat once cautioned David about using slurs to describe the poor, hard-working "colored" people on the streets below. Both parents, in fact, issued explicit instructions to substitute "tiger" for the derogatory racial epithet in the rhythmic chant Bronx boys invoked when choosing up for teams in street games.

Broad mindedness, however, had limits. As Dorothy and four-year-old David had taken a stroll one day, an older woman stopped to admire the youngster's dark skin and curly hair and wondered what a lovely boy like that was doing in the neighborhood, leading Dorothy aghast that the bystander had mistaken her son for a Negro.

A confrontation with Joe, the huge, gruff, slow-moving building janitor who wore oversized overalls and never spoke a word, offered another case of racial tension. One Saturday afternoon after Christmas, Nat had brought David down to the basement workroom to watch him attach the tracks of a newly acquired Lionel electric train set onto a large piece of plywood. Needing an additional tool from the apartment, he told the boy to wait until he returned. Moments later, Joe shuffled out of his living quarters. Cursing under his breath about the pounding that had interrupted his weekend nap, he ripped the plywood off the workbench.

Taken aback by the resounding crash, David channeled rising fear and outrage into a hefty kick to the culprit's rear. This only fed Joe's fury. Uttering incomprehensible threats under his breath as he slowly advanced with outstretched hands, the giant man stalked the screaming and panic-stricken youngster halfway down the dimly lit basement corridor.

Just at that point, Nat emerged from the elevator. "I left you alone for two minutes!" he scolded in a fit of exasperation mixed with fear.

Opening in 1950, the Sedgwick Houses included nine buildings, each fifteen stories, to serve nearly eight hundred families, many of them Puerto Rican and African American. How much changing neighborhood demographics influenced the decision to seek a suburban haven is difficult to say. In any case, Sundays now began with a perusal of the *New York Times* real estate section and excursions to the world of suburbia.

Whether new or used, Nat required that any property had to feature mature trees and greenery, have a fireplace, and be located in a predominantly Jewish area with a synagogue in the vicinity. For her part, Dorothy insisted on three bedrooms and a clean, spacious, and modern kitchen with room for a table and chairs to seat four. Most important, she insisted upon a solid structure that did not recall the seediness of Lake Huntington.

Faith

Although weekend drives to Long Island, Westchester County, and northern New Jersey resulted in several "earnest money" deposits on appealing homes, Nat could not bring himself to take on mortgage debt. In the end, his Depression rooted anxiety generated a compromise —the family would wait for a two-bedroom apartment to open up at 1495 in anticipation of larger cash reserves while continuing to spend summers in the Catskills. Sure enough, just before retrieving Dorothy and the boys from the mountains after Labor Day in 1951, Nat moved the family up a floor to apartment 3-J. The view from the western exposure of the airy four-room unit extended to the top of the eastern tower of the George Washington Bridge, and on particularly clear days, to a glimpse of the distant Palisades along the Hudson River past the northern tip of Manhattan.

Nat and Dorothy chose the bedroom facing the courtyard by the front door. This meant that David and Michael could share a bright room by the fire escape window, where they each had their own bed, desk, and dresser. The living room, with mustard painted walls replicating the cover of a favorite Chopin record album, sported a matching rug, two colorful prints of a Bruegel wedding scene, and an inside wall for the piano. "*Schlermie*"—a table lamp with a carved figure of an old street lamplighter—stood out among the room's cozy Early American furnishings.

The move to new quarters corresponded with David's first term in Hebrew School. In a marriage that fused Orthodox tradition and agnostic secularism, the family celebrated both Hanukkah and Christmas. During the Jewish Festival of Lights, Nat illuminated the ceremonial Hanukkah candles, recited the appropriate blessings, and saw that everyone had ample stocks of Becky's tasty potato *latkes*, whose secret recipe depended upon a generous mix of onions. On Christmas morning, in turn, the boys received presents like most American children their age.

The Jewish High Holidays—the New Year and Day of Atonement—provided special meaning for Nat. Yet an explicit understanding allowed Dorothy to stay at home while the boys accompanied their dad on the half-mile walk to the Orthodox *shul* (synagogue) – the five-story Hebrew Institute of University Heights. For Nat, worship on the holidays brought back the rituals and traditions of youth. Nothing pleased him more than to bring David and Michael to Becky's camp chair in the women's section of the auxiliary assembly hall, a low-ceiling, over-heated chamber that spared older congregants the large flight of stairs to the main sanctuary. As bearded, white-robed elders in sneakers conducted the service in a steady drone amid a constant buzz, the proud Horowitz matriarch would bestow fervent kisses and hugs upon her grandsons.

On afternoon breaks, Nat led the boys on long walks across the Harlem River on the (Little) Washington Bridge. He told them that Orthodox Jews customarily cast their sins onto the waters on the Day of Atonement, although he showed no inclination to do so himself and kept his personal beliefs to himself. The subject of Nazi death camps and the mass murder of European Jews, although widely known, never surfaced in family discussion. Yet Nat always urged his sons to never forget who they were and to maintain pride in their Jewish heritage.

A favorite family snapshot pictured eight-year-old David in a new Passover suit and fedora hat with a Hebrew prayer book and *talis* prayer scarf in hand. A key part of Dorothy's arrangement with Nat stipulated that both boys would attend Hebrew School for three years to develop the reading knowledge of Hebrew and understanding of religious history and culture to qualify them for the *Bar-Mitzvah* ceremony marking the transition to Jewish adulthood.

David's attendance at Hebrew School late Monday through Thursday afternoons and Sunday mornings during the fall of 1951 occurred just as he became a devoted New York Giants fan. Baseball was a serious matter in a city then hosting the Yankees, Giants, and Brooklyn Dodgers. Nat had become a Giant follower in the 1920s when the team included Jewish second baseman Andy Cohen. He continued to root for the Giants through the 1940s when Sid Gordon, a Brooklyn-born Jew, starred as the squad's power hitter. Formerly a Yankee fan and admirer of home run slugger Babe Ruth, Dorothy had "converted" to her husband's team even before the marriage. It would not have occurred to David to choose a different path any more than he would have announced he had become a Christian. Yet rooting for the Giants was a challenge in a neighborhood only a mile from Yankee Stadium, a circumstance made more difficult by the unpromising performance of the family favorites through most of that legendary season.

By mid-August, the Giants were thirteen-and-a-half games behind the first-place Dodgers, only to stage one of the greatest comebacks in baseball history. Tying Brooklyn for the National League lead on the last day of the season, the Giants forced a three-game post-season playoff. Not long after David raced home from school to follow the third and deciding game on television, however, the Dodgers surged ahead by a score of 4-1 with a top of the ninth inning rally. Her son's pain seemed too much for Dorothy to bear. Acting on the same impulse that she demonstrated when he had experienced a terrible day and she urged him to go to bed for a fresh start in the morning, she persuaded him to take off for Hebrew School to cut short the misery.

A completely deflated David complied. Yet some time later amid an Israeli songfest on the top floor of the Hebrew Institute, he heard a commotion at the door.

It was Dorothy with Mikey in tow, nearly out of breath after racing the half-mile down University Avenue and sprinting up four flights of stairs.

"Davey, Davey!" she screamed across the crowded gym floor.

"Davey, Davey!" she repeated.

"The Giants won! The Giants won! They won! They won the pennant!"

Seconds later, she had him in her arms as the threesome leaped for joy across the creaky floor. According to Dorothy's recollection, the bearded elderly cantor, helpless to control the ensuing bedlam, adjusted his glasses and quietly exclaimed, "The Lord Be Praised!"

The Giants had staged the ultimate bottom-of-the-ninth-inning comeback highlighted by third baseman Bobby Thomson's pennant-winning three-run home run. Dorothy would always feel guilty for depriving her son of the most iconic moment of baseball history. In retrospect, she tried to say she had acted out of respect for her husband's commitment to a Jewish education. Yet Dorothy's instincts were far more likely to have been more protective than severe.

Hollywood Blvd.

Although Nat and Dorothy incorporated strong doses of emotional support and compassion in their parenting, they never stinted on high expectations. Each of the boys had the responsibility of making his own bed in the morning and picking up after himself. Everyone was to turn out electric lights when leaving a room. No food was to be wasted. Disrespect for parental authority could merit a spanking. Diligence in schoolwork, moreover, was a necessity.

Michael excelled in his classes and never asked for help. Yet David sometimes called on his father for assistance in tasks such as constructing a village of African cardboard huts, assembling an erector set frame for a covered wagon, or gluing together plastic antique model cars. Beyond that, Nat liked to remind his older son that he could have the rest of the weekend free if he completed his homework on Friday night. He also pressed David to turn B+ grades into A's by avoiding careless errors. To emphasize the point, the West sales representative brought home an inspirational "THINK" desk placard from IBM, one of his new clients.

Summers in the Catskills offered a welcome respite from these responsibilities. As the 1952 season approached, however, twenty families organized a collective walkout from Strolowitz's Bungalows when the owner declined to build a swimming pool. The group now relocated to Fink's Kauneonga Park near White Lake. The clean and tidy cabins were a five-minute walk to the water and an ample swimming dock. The colony also boasted a newly constructed softball field with a screened backstop, freshly tar-surfaced tennis and shuffleboard courts, a handball court, a knotty-pine paneled casino, a canteen (general store) with a pinball machine and full soda fountain, and plans for a pool. Sidney Fink sealed the agreement by promising that his hefty seventeen-year-old son would take center field for the men's softball squad, for which lefty place hitter Nat Horowitz played first base.

Passing on the more expensive rentals in "Skunk Hollow," Nat and Dorothy reserved a unit on the recently constructed "Hollywood Boulevard." Despite their mundane cinder block construction, stucco siding, flat roofs, and lack of screened porches, the semi-attached row of bungalows boasted "Hollywood kitchens" with built-in appliances and ample cupboards as well as knotty-pine paneling throughout. Besides, the couple chose a location on the quiet end of the complex adjoining the nearby woods and the cawing of crows in the morning. As a sales representative who made his own hours, Nat arrived for weekends on early Friday afternoon and did not leave for the City until seven on Monday morning. This entitled him to three early swims in the brisk waters of Kauneonga Lake, a ritual that often culminated in a trip to the local bakery to bring home fresh poppy-seed bagels and breakfast jellyrolls.

Like most Catskill bungalow colonies, whose rates were far below those of the upscale hotels, the Fink compound mainly attracted working-class families from the East Bronx and the Flatbush district of Brooklyn. Nat was completely at home with the Jewish garment workers and tradesmen who made up the colony's residents. Cigar chomping George Klein, a Bronx candy distributor who returned to the City to refill his vending machines once a week, functioned as the unofficial police officer of the community and played outfield on the men's softball team. Star pitcher and slugger Pip Slugh added to his talents on the field with movie star looks and a joke for every occasion. Indeed, most of the colony's denizens loved hearing a well-told Yiddish story. It was not surprising, then, that Kauneonga Lake offered the perfect setting for Nady Horowitz's return to his roots in Yiddish theatrics.

During the summer of 1953, Nat took on the task of writing and directing a "mock marriage" for an adults-only, amateur production.

Mock marriages were salacious theatrical farces that incorporated Yiddish and English send-ups of popular and ethnic songs into a burlesque of the Jewish wedding ceremony. The extravaganza's raucous humor rested upon the fact that male performers cross-dressed as women (including the inevitably pregnant bride) and that their female counterparts portrayed the leering rabbi, the reluctant groom, and other colorful figures. Casting complete amateurs in the show only added to the appeal.

After several weekends of arduous rehearsals, Nady's crew of bungalow colony non-professionals made its theatrical debut on a humid Saturday night in August. Once friends and neighbors settled into their seats in the overcrowded casino, the show opened with the "rabbi's" entreaty for "the congregation" to take its place to the tune of a traditional Yiddish melody:

> *Menchelech, menchelech,*
> *Zets sich oif de benchelech.*

From there, the proceedings descended into slapstick hilarity and a bawdy mockery of the matrimonial ritual, including a good deal of off-color humor addressing the sexual propensities or inadequacies of the principals. The final number presented an upbeat parody of the popular song, "Civilization" (1947), reworked for the Fink's crowd:

> Bonga, bonga, bonga,
> It's so nice in Kauneonga,
> Oh, ho, ho, ho, ho.
>
> Bingle, bingle, bingle,
> I am such a happy *yingle*
> I refuse to go.
>
> Give me the country, green trees,
> Herring, cream cheese,
> I make it clear,
> That no matter how they nudge me,
> I'll stay right here.

For an audience that seldom had the chance to attend Broadway productions, the mock marriage was top-rate entertainment. Nady later claimed that several top Catskills resorts offered him lucrative fees for the rights although he always declined the proposals.

Tin Waltz

Dorothy tolerated summers in the Catskills out of deference to her husband and the boys but missed the cultural refinements of the City. She always had insisted that raising a family would not interfere with creative activities or appreciation of the arts. Each Saturday afternoon, live broadcasts of New York's Metropolitan Opera on WQXR, the classical music voice of the *New York Times*, emanated from the living room or car radio. Meanwhile, long-playing records of Haydn, Mozart, Beethoven, Schubert, and other favorites filled the shelves of a converted dining room server. Dinner invites to Charlie Kingsford, moreover, usually culminated in impromptu classical piano concerts. Even the boys contributed to the mix—David with a well-practiced piece at the keyboard, Michael with dramatic recitations of works such as Christopher Morley's light verse, "Animal Crackers."

For her part, Dorothy continued to pursue literary aspirations. Some of her poetry addressed ambivalent feelings about motherhood and domesticity. A short story, "The Sitter," portrays a harried mother who imagines she is the wife of a short, fat, and balding neighbor. Seeking to refurbish intellectual energies, Dorothy returned to Hunter College for Wednesday night classes in January 1954. Ingeniously, she sold Nat on the idea by pointing out that she could supplement the boys' college fund with a professional teaching certificate. Left to their own devices, the Horowitz men made do with kosher deli take-out suppers of cold tongue, corned beef, and pastrami sandwiches on rye or Russian black bread served with potato salad, coleslaw, sour pickles, and Dr. Brown's Cel-Ray Tonic or Cream Soda. In later years, however, Dorothy recalled that some women neighbors had responded to her quest for autonomy by gossiping that her husband's paycheck "wasn't good enough for her."

During the winter of 1954 Nathan and Dorothy focused on the play they had begun writing six years earlier. Originally called "Fortune in Men's Eyes" after a line from a Shakespearean sonnet, the work received a 1949 copyright with Dorothy and Nat Harris listed as co-authors. Yet with the completion of an initial draft the following year, the title shifted to "Pipe Dream" under the name Nat Harris.

With distinct autobiographical overtones, "Pipe Dream" portrayed a retail shoe clerk who yearns to fulfill a lifelong desire to be a creative force as a classical music composer.

"I sell shoes because we have to eat," Paul explains, but "there's always the frustrated feeling that you were meant for bigger things."

The story turns on a visit from an old pal who has married a talented playwright and become a successful Broadway producer.

Hank "used to think me the most talented guy alive," Paul assures his wife Phyllis.

Taking advantage of the friendship, the aspiring composer pleads for a chance to score incidental music for Hank's new production. Yet this does not sit well with Phyllis, who sees her husband's fixation as an unrealistic venture that threatens the family's financial security.

"We're not starry-eyed kids anymore," she explains. "How long can you play the artist in the garret?"

Although Phyllis correctly senses that Paul has limited talent, a soliloquy by a meek fellow shoe store clerk and neighbor offers a graphic picture of life without inspiration:

> Our whole lives are spent in boxes ... Apartments are nothing but boxes strung together. In the morning, I leave my box – and go to the big box, the store. I take the little box – the elevator – up to the shoe department, and there I'm completely surrounded by boxes – with shoes in them. When the day is done, I reverse the whole procedure and come back to the box I started from... And what's the wind-up of it all – the permanent box, the final dust-collector.

At the same time, as Paul struggles to compose an original score, he passes on his frustration to his young daughter, who he has forced to take piano lessons (she even monitors her practice time with an alarm clock!)

"All of us have such terrific egos," Phyllis observes. "If our children aren't shining lights, it makes us just miserable."

Paul's rage at his daughter's lack of interest in her lessons leads to a confrontation with her piano teacher. A refugee from wartime Germany whose daughter had been a concert pianist before perishing in a Nazi concentration camp, she insists that love of music must come spontaneously, not out of the desire to please a parent or anyone else.

In the end, Paul comes to acknowledge his wife's admonition that "small talents are for living rooms." More to the point, he comes to appreciate the wisdom of his daughter's mentor.

"You are trying to fight insignificance," the instructor tells Paul. Instead, she urges him to accept the possibility that love of family and enjoyment of fine music for its own sake can mark a fulfilling existence.

After all, she points out, "we need people behind counters, people to deliver milk, pave roads."

Not long after the initial completion of "Pipe Dream," highly acclaimed playwright William Inge agreed to review the work in confidence.

"This is a good play," reported Inge. "It holds together, the characterizations are sound and interesting, and the story moves."

Yet the author of *Come Back, Little Sheba* (1950) feared that the message that 'we can't all be performers' was "too worn to be specifically treated now." Besides, he thought the play explained too much without letting the audience experience what the author intended and regretted that the writing style lacked irony. A second obstacle surfaced when a letter from attorneys for Richard Rodgers and Oscar Hammerstein warned that the musical comedy team had a show named *Pipe Dream* scheduled for a Broadway debut. Without the resources to fight high-powered lawyers, Nat Harris reluctantly changed the name to *Tin Waltz*.

After years of persistent effort, the play finally found a home. With Bessie Levine and Teddy Mass serving as financial angels, "off-Broadway's" Actors and Writers Theater mounted a ten-day production of the drama in a church basement on West 46th Street in April 1954. Opening night produced an enthusiastic crowd of relatives, friends, and neighbors and a tide of congratulatory telegrams. Yet the critical reviews were not encouraging. *Show Business* acknowledged the "emotionally affecting moments" of the production but thought the script suffered from facile characterizations and a pat resolution. *The New York Times* dismissed the play as a "dolorous tale...rickety in its structure and vague in its insight."

Tin Waltz would not "move east of Eighth Avenue," predicted *Variety*.

July 24, 1954

In one of his less generous frames of mind, Nat would attribute the financial and artistic failure of *Tin Waltz* to "deviates, homosexuals, and lesbians" in the theater company to whom he attributed little understanding of "normal" families. In truth, the project fell outside the author's talent for poignant sketches, dialect caricatures, comic parodies, and playful rhymes.

"I never strove for language unfamiliar to my tongue," Nat subsequently noted. Yet much of the *Tin Waltz* dialogue suffered from the excessively redundant and moralistic voice of 1930s political agitprop. If that criticism holds water, it may be that Dorothy had a larger hand in the work's composition than the sole copyright suggested. In helping to render the story of an ordinary man's struggle to achieve distinction, had a loving wife sought to offer her husband a subtle form of adjustment therapy? If so, the effort backfired. Defensive about the response to his talents, Nat could barely watch another TV play or comic routine without venting hyper-criticism. The uncanny replica of the bitterness shown by *Tin Waltz*'s main character mirrored the cynicism that Nat Horowitz often projected upon a seemingly hostile world.

Fortunately, preparations for David's coming *Bar-Mitzvah* ceremony served as a healthy distraction, as did another summer at Fink's Bungalows. One of the leading attractions of the season involved the highly competitive matches the men's softball team played each Saturday. On July 24th, however, as the squad prepared for a showdown against a neighboring colony, Nat and Dorothy decided to visit Becky, who was escaping the New York heat at a cluster of cottages near the Catskills town of Liberty. Not wanting to miss the game, both boys remained on the grounds.

When David trotted out to the outfield to shag fly balls during pre-game warm-ups, he heard the loudspeaker summon George Klein to the telephone. Not long after, he noticed several other key players were nowhere in sight. Something must be up, he thought.

Then David heard one of the fielders behind him say his parents were on their way home.

This innocuous piece of information proved to be extremely significant because minutes later, he heard someone ask whether his mother and father "were still alive."

Shortly before 2 p.m., a milk truck traveling south on Route 17 had lost its air brakes as it descended the mountain slope to downtown Liberty. At 60 mph, the vehicle careened down three blocks of Main Street, ramming into eleven autos and two trucks before it smashed into a stonewall, overturned, and burst into flames. Within seconds, three people lost their lives and another fourteen suffered substantial injuries.

Nat and Dorothy had been waiting for a traffic light in the midst of the business district. Ironically, they were on the way to an auto supply store to find new seat covers for the Studebaker. Sitting in the passenger seat, Dorothy was a helpless witness to the entire nightmare.

To her horror, one of the front fenders of the upside-down and decimated milk truck wound up barely touching the driver's side of the Studebaker's front hood.

"This is it," Nat remembered thinking.

Overcoming immediate shock, the dutiful husband had the presence of mind to get his wife out of the car. Then he rushed to another vehicle to find other victims, only to discover a dead male passenger in the back seat.

That evening, Nat took David for a quiet walk in the brush beyond left field. In a subdued voice, he explained he had silently recited the "*kaddish*" prayer for the departed in recognition of the close brush with death he and Dorothy had experienced.

Hours later, Nat finally broke down in the privacy of the shower.

The insurance settlement from the totaled Studebaker helped pay for a new black and red, four-door Mercury sedan with matching vinyl seats. Such extravagance was out of character for the cost-conscious Horowitz family, but Dorothy was in need of a larger vehicle to enhance her compromised sense of security. Although a radio broadcast initially had identified the couple as fatalities, neither had received a scratch. Yet the experience traumatized Dorothy, who was upset that she had curled up into a fetal position with no apparent concern for her husband's welfare. Seeing a therapist back in New York, she learned that her reaction had been a natural survival mechanism. To overcome her sense of powerlessness and to assume control over her own fate, the psychologist recommended she learn to drive and complete her teacher training.

Dorothy passed the New York City instructor's license exam in the fall of 1954, allowing her to serve as a substitute teacher while finishing coursework. As a reminder of the transient nature of life and her good fortune, she had a replica license plate of the Studebaker mounted on a tiny metal model of a yellow milk truck, a fixture she never removed from her desk. For years, however, even the sound of a large rig's air brakes caused her palms to break out in sweat.

Bess

Following David's *Bar-Mitzvah* ceremony in September, one hundred friends and family gathered at a University Avenue catering hall for a meal featuring the guest of honor's favorites—roast turkey, cranberry sauce, mashed potatoes, green peas, iced tea, and chocolate layer cake. True to form, Nat composed his son's welcoming remarks with instructions on the proper pronunciation of the obligatory Yiddish asides and the pacing of laugh lines. A month later, the family celebrated the first New York Giants baseball championship in twenty-one years.

On New Year's Eve, however, thirteen-year-old David began to move out of his parents' orbit. Although comic books, tabloid papers such as the *New York Daily News,* and attendance at violent movies were taboo in the Horowitz household, popular music had always been part of the family scene. Both the Strolowitz and Fink bungalow colony loudspeakers broadcast the hits of the day, and Dorothy regularly tuned into the Arthur Godfrey morning variety radio show and other programs. Once David completed his Saturday morning classical music piano lesson, moreover, Nat made a habit of treating him to two sheet music selections of popular hits at the Carl Fisher Store across 57th Street.

When a friend exposed David to rock 'n' roll music on a New Year's Eve radio program, however, family dynamics entered a new era. The sexually charged metaphors and earthy rhythms of the genre were offensive to parents who cherished the harmonies of classical music and the sophisticated creations of the Jewish Tin Pan Alley tunesmiths. In contrast to the cultural refinement Nat and Dorothy favored, the primitive tone of southern and working-class blues shouters seemed coarse and threatening. David did not help matters when he insisted on listening to the radio as he finished homework and dried the after-dinner dishes.

Nevertheless, when David became a rock 'n' roll fanatic during the spring of 1955, Nathan and Dorothy had other things on their mind. By now, Nat was paying frequent visits to see Pip Slugh, who lay helpless in a Brooklyn hospital with terminal lung cancer.

"He's wasting away," Nat whispered to his wife during a late-night kitchen confab. "Dotty, there's nothing left but skin and bones."

Pip died well before summer, inspiring Dorothy to initiate a campaign to put an end to the pack a day of Chesterfield cigarettes Nat had begun smoking after giving up his pipe at the defense plant. Almost daily, she taped news articles on the bathroom mirror detailing the links between smoking and cancer. When Nat used the advent of a flu bug to break the habit, the strategy succeeded. Yet by the time it did, Dorothy was dealing with her mother.

Following a trip to the gambling resort of Havana, Cuba that January, Bess Levine complained of back aches and saw a chiropractor. Unrelieved of her discomfort by spring, she experienced indigestion and intestinal pains. The doctors eventually diagnosed her with pancreatic cancer, for which cobalt radiation treatments proved futile. While Becky stayed with David and Michael at Fink's Bungalows during the summer of 1955 and Nat came up for weekends, Dorothy remained in New York..

At 6:30 on the morning of August 31st, Sidney Fink knocked softly on the bungalow door with a summons to the telephone.

"O.K. boys," Nat announced upon returning minutes later. "We've got to get up and pack to go home."

Only the night before, David and Michael had learned that Bess was nearing the end and that they might have to leave for New York at any time. As the three rode in silence down Route 17, everyone understood they were abandoning the mountains for the last time. The widely attended funeral service reflected Bess Levine's thirty-five year involvement in politics and social activism. Following her service in the Socialist Party, Bess had founded and continued to serve as an officer of the Women's Auxiliary of the American Veterans Committee, Mickey's most important affiliation. She also had been an executive committee member of the powerful West Side Branch of Americans for Democratic Action, the chapter Mickey had chaired, and a leading figure in New York's Liberal Party. Newbold Morris, an anti-Tammany Hall civic campaigner and Levine admirer, delivered the eulogy.

Exodus

Acutely aware of Bess's problematic marriage, Dorothy had a difficult time with her death. When the boys returned to the Bronx, Nat led Michael into a room to see his mother, where he discovered her playing solitaire with a vacant stare on her face. That fall, Dorothy underwent surgery to remove a benign growth from her thyroid gland. She then experienced a bout of depression likely triggered by her disrupted hormones and recent loss. At home, she fixated on Frank Sinatra's *In the Wee Small Hours*, an album of melancholy torch songs.

Nat Levine, long freed of the Whitehall, now came to the apartment for Friday evening dinners following visits to the racetrack. When he had done well, he would slip the boys five-dollar bills. If he were unduly quiet, his son-in-law would invariably notice.

"What's the matter, Grandpa?" Nat Horowitz would tease, "bad day at the track?"

On Veteran's Day weekend of 1955, the Horowitz and Levine families gathered in Atlantic City for the ninth annual convention of AVC, now nearly thirty thousand strong. The occasion marked Mickey's installation as national chair and the inauguration of the Bessie Levine service award. That winter, AVC's new leader conducted a one-man inquiry into Veterans Administration discrimination against Negro clients in five southern states and summarized his findings in a biting 2,500-word report to the House Veterans Affairs Committee.

In the wake of Bess's death, Dorothy toyed with the idea of sharing a large house with her brother and father. Yet Nat's taste for gracious older homes and her preference for a modern kitchen had eliminated several possibilities by the spring of 1956. At that point, Nat Levine made a surprise announcement.

"You know how I loved your mother and still miss her," he addressed Dorothy and Mickey. Then he said he was going to remarry and move to Florida.

His son and daughter sat in stony silence. Nat Horowitz offered the only response. "At a certain age," he observed quietly, "a person has a right to companionship."

Weeks later on an errand at Macy's, he ran into the former Julie Kaminsky (now Kaye), a Compensation Clinic cohort from the Thirties. Julie and his family lived in a Long Island complex of seven hundred residences known as the Country Club Homes. Constructed in 1950 as an upscale version of Levittown in newly named Roslyn Heights, the development mirrored the modernist designs of architect Frank Lloyd Wright. Its low-hanging eaves, wood-framed floor-to-ceiling windows, brick-walled corner fireplaces, natural pine interiors, and flowing floor plans combined a rustic feel with contemporary lines.

Lacking basements, the homes were set on concrete slabs with water-heated electric coils beneath tiled floors. Dorothy marveled at the automatic washer, dryer and dishwasher in the efficient and spacious kitchen and the luxury of two full bathrooms. Nat admired the landscaped third-of-an-acre plots nestled comfortably among the community's winding streets, reminding him of scenes from a Currier and Ives print. He also relished the varied mix of exterior materials and lot orientations that provided a unique look to each property. The Olympic-size swimming pool at the "country club" added another plus.

Not long after, a single-story Country Club ranch came on the market. Besides a cheerful and easy-to-clean kitchen, the house at 45 Carriage Lane incorporated natural wood into much of its cabinetry, its storage attic stairway, and the swinging bookcase separating the dining area from an optional third bedroom. Within walking distance of two synagogues—one Conservative and one Reform—a Jewish bakery, and a kosher supermarket, and boasting two apple trees and several pines in the backyard, the place seemed to meet every demand.

Julie advised that the $25,500 list price was competitive and warned that homes in the area never stayed on the market very long. The only question was the mortgage.

"What would Dotty and the kids do if something happened to me?" Nat wondered during several sleepless nights.

Buying a house, he later acknowledged, "was like looking down from a high board."

Nevertheless, as Nat subsequently explained in an autobiographical short story, Dorothy had "swept beyond the horizon of the Bronx" for years. Responding to her quiet insistence, he finally summoned the courage to cast Depression anxieties aside and sign on to a twenty-four year, 4 percent interest rate note.

He once recalled the couple leaving the lawyer's office, "clutching each other's hand, exaltation, anxiety, and fear clutching their heart."

On July 17, 1956, David and Michael posed for a snapshot behind the back of a moving van and took leave of Popham Avenue. Borrowing

Nat Levine's Ford Fairlane, Mickey took his nephews upstate to visit the Baseball Hall of Fame. Meanwhile, Nat and Dorothy managed the transition to new quarters. By the time the boys returned, the interior of the house had undergone a complete overall. Instead of its green carpet and walls, the layout now featured familiar earth tones and Early American furnishings. Up from Miami, Nat Levine helped his son-in-law complete a last minute wallpapering job on the master bedroom at 3:30 in the morning.

Between 1945 and 1960, nineteen million American families relocated to the suburbs. By the end of that period, a majority of the nation's households owned their own homes. For the Horowitz clan, the move to Long Island marked the culmination of a historic migration rooted in the shtetls of Eastern Europe and the proletarian quarters of the Lower East Side and East Bronx. With renewed confidence in their prospects and vision of the good life, Nat and Dorothy set caution aside and looked to assume their place in the middle class.

5

THIS SIDE OF PARADISE

Once Nat Horowitz became a homeowner in the summer of 1956, he took immense pride in the wholesome, cheerful, and safe environment suburban life offered his family. As a product of the "teeming Bronx ghetto," as he once described it, he nearly wept when he saw the brand new sprawling Wheatley junior and senior high school his sons would attend. For her part, Dorothy had outgrown the provincial world of the West Bronx. With a permanent teaching certificate and driver's license in hand and a second-hand Oldsmobile now at her disposal, she looked forward to the fall, when she would be leading a fifth grade class in Corona, Queens. At the same time, she continued pursuing a graduate education degree in evening courses at Queens College. For her as well, the comfortably furnished but unpretentious rustic home in Roslyn Heights served as a haven from a world too often given to crass preoccupations and ostentatious display.

Refuge

Intent on acclimating David and Michael to the suburbs before the house closed in mid-July, Dorothy drove the boys from the Bronx to the Country Club pool each early summer weekday afternoon. Once the move to Roslyn Heights took place, the boys received sleek new "English-style" bikes. Slow to make new friends, however, they spent most of the time at the back-patio picnic table engrossed in a baseball board game. Frustrated that the suburban idyll had come to this, Dorothy exploded in frustration one day and ripped the set to shreds.

Apart from the twenty-mile commute to Manhattan on the Long Island Expressway, Nat had little difficulty in adjusting to suburban existence. Relishing the surrounding greenery, he believed he had entered what he later described as "this side of Paradise."

"Digging my hands into the soil and the odor of grass cutting," he would recall, "brought out the perhaps inherent yearnings for the earth within me."

Dorothy would have preferred spending most of her time quietly reading. In contrast, Nat enjoyed inviting old Bronx friends and neighbors to show off his new home and engage in informal socializing or "*schmoozing*." Occasionally, Bernie and Teddy Mass, now apartment residents in the upscale Riverdale section of the North Bronx, visited, as did Charlie Kingsford. Nat and Dorothy even provided a friendly ear for a loquacious appliance repairer who preferred their company to immediately returning to his wife and family at the end of a long workday.

Uncle Mickey was by far the most frequent guest. Now an executive assistant and fundraiser at New York's Federation of Jewish Philanthropies, Mickey delighted in entertaining his brother-in-law with the latest rabbinical jokes. A favorite concerned Sadie Rubinstein and the haughty telephone caller who asks if he has reached the "Anderson residence."

"*Oi*, mister," she responds, "do you have the wrong number!"

The response became a favorite household one-liner.

Mickey shared a passion for musical theater with the entire family. Following an exposé detailing a Broadway scalping scandal in 1949, Nat had secured tickets for an opening week performance of Rodgers and Hammerstein's *South Pacific*, an ultimate Pulitzer Prize winner.

Highlights from leading musicals eventually took their place alongside the classical works in the family's long-playing record collection. Although Nat leaned toward the romantic themes of *Brigadoon* and *Kismet* and Dorothy admired the strong female characters in *Annie Get Your Gun* and *The King and I*, Mickey's tastes revolved around the social satire and witty phrasing of a *Finian's Rainbow*, *Fiorello! Three-penny Opera*, or *My Fair Lady*.

From musical comedy, conversation could range from the evils of southern racial segregation to Tammany Hall corruption to the sins of Stalinist repression and the late dictator's American defenders. Matters of religion also attracted attention. Observing the traditions and rituals that gave continuity to his life, Nat presided over abbreviated versions of the annual Passover *Seder*, assisted by Michael during occasional bursts of Judaic fervor. Everyone remained respectful during the boys' recitation of the "Four Questions." Yet references to the Ten Plagues imposed on the Egyptians seldom passed without commentary.

"Nat, that's a wonderfully compassionate God you worship," Mickey would tease. Dorothy would then plead for no mention of locusts or pestilence before dinner.

Outnumbered, Nat usually surrendered with good cheer.

"O.K., let's eat now, folks," he would announce to everyone's delight.

Corona

Five months before her fortieth birthday, Dorothy inaugurated her full-time teaching career at P. S. 186. Drawing upon an extensive range of reading and a longstanding familiarity with the arts, she devised original lessons plans to reach the working-class Irish and Italian American students who dominated her classroom. One outline became the basis of a graduate course presentation she entitled "How to launch a 4th grade social studies unit." The package refashioned "I Like New York," one of Dorothy's poetic tributes to Karl Marx, poet Carl Sandburg, and orchestra conductor Arturo Toscanini from the 1930s, into a latter-day celebration of polio vaccine creator Jonas Salk and musical maestro Leonard Bernstein.

For the next five years, Dorothy threw herself into a variety of school activities that included service as faculty adviser to the Student Council and school newspaper, leadership of the Staff Relations and Guidance committees, and coordinator of teacher training. "ME," a poem written for an instructional staff meeting, encouraged her colleagues to see the best in students:

> There is a me I'd like to be,
> A smiling, friendly busy me,
> That's the me, I'd like to be!
>
> . . . .
>
> Please forget the things I did,
> When I was a noisy, silly kid,
> Just remember I spelled so well,
> And never ran out before the bell.
>
> When my teachers talk to me,
> How I hope that they will see,
> What a really fine person I can be!
> That's the me,
> I'd like to be!

Dorothy's empathy emerged in "Every Day," a short story depicting the bleakness of poverty rendered through the eyes of a lonely street urchin:

> Every day my bigger brother wakes me up. He punches me in the head. We sleep in the same bed in the hall. He punches me in the head. And I wake up every day....I go downstairs to play. I wish I had a bike... I kick away some garbage and sit down on the stoop. I pick up a tin can and try to hit the hydrant. I'm a good pitcher. Every day I get better!

As a teacher, Dorothy readily understood that student performance often reflected conditions outside the institution. In families where single or divorced mothers had to work outside the home, for example, little opportunity existed for monitoring school work, particularly in overcrowded quarters. More severe problems could include parental alcoholism or physical abuse. Following up her interest in psychology, she began to shape her college graduate program into preparation for a guidance-counseling certificate.

Westwinds

Nat often praised his wife's career, which he compared favorably to the unbridled commercialism of the newly renamed West Chemical. He particularly dreaded the Christmas season, when the sales crew had to spend hundreds of dollars of their own funds on client gifts (a bottle of Scotch for most of the men, perfume or premium candy for the women). Nat also felt obligated to protect his roster of customers from in-house poaching. Distrustful of the front office, he enlisted Dorothy's monthly help in checking the pink carbon copies of sales receipts to make sure the firm had given him full credit for his commissions.

Whatever the downside of a life dedicated to selling amid the pressure of monthly mortgage payments and bills, Nat Harris took pride in his success. No wonder he declined company offers to "promote" him to district sales manager at a salary that would have amounted to far less than his commissions. Although he rarely called attention to it, Nat Harris had developed a distinctive way of pursuing his craft. Discovering the utility of a low-key and relaxed approach free of sales banter, backslapping, or overselling, he learned to inspire an enormous amount of trust among clients in the most cutthroat business climate in the country.

"Nat, just tell me what I need," customers often responded when the West man inquired about the status of their washroom and cleaning supplies.

If a potential customer complained about the company's high prices, Nat would point out that the quality of West products outpaced the competition and would save money in the end. If a patron had issues with the timeliness of a service contract, Nat's personal word suggested an imminent resolution of the matter. In some cases, repeat customers became friends—some even wound up soliciting advice on how to deal with troubled teenagers or other issues.

Responding to a management request in 1958, Nat Harris began compiling a monthly inspirational column for *Westwinds*, the firm's national house organ. Whatever his feeling toward superiors, the assignment offered an opportunity to incorporate the writing talents he had nurtured since boyhood with the business experience gained from twelve years "pounding the pavements," as he liked to describe it.

"The years have been a patient teacher," an early piece advised in a segment devoted to following up completed sales.

"I have learned that an order is only an order when it is safely sanctioned."

"Had I waited for this one to come fluttering safely to me, the insect life in this brewery would have flourished and eventually found representation in the best basements of New York."

"My duty as a civic-minded citizen was to corral this order for the good of my customer, the city, and incidentally, my son's college fund."

One *Westwinds* column recalled an inquiry from a respectful newcomer about the knack of selling. After thinking of all the sterile bromides favored by management, Nat's answer resonated with his easygoing sale personality.

'Just lucky, fella, just lucky,' he replied.

An entry entitled "Diary of a West Day" asked if anyone realized "what an interesting trail the West man sniffs on?"

It then presented a litany often repeated at home:

> Your contacts have ranged from porters to presidents. Your shoes have accumulated the dust from cellars to the down of plush broadloom. Your personality has been flexibly attuned to every challenging situation.

The selection then listed a variety of clients from a Bronx fish market to the manager of the largest city housing project to a Times Square dance school to a funeral home in Harlem. In later years, Nat would bring major concerns like the Port Authority of New York, several large hospitals, and the national headquarters of Jehovah's Witnesses into his sales portfolio.

"Being a West salesman in this great metropolis is a unique experience," he declared in another column.

Indeed, Nat Harris's columns were remarkable in insisting that the inspiration for selling stemmed from more than hunger for earnings. In a passage that hovered between self-revelation and motivational cheerleading, he listed the desire for prestige, a positive self-image, and a sense of accomplishment as the foundations of a successful sales career.

After "the prospect, the pounding, the grinding," he wrote, one could experience "the wonderful pervasive warmth of a realized fruition."

"From the inception of an idea to its living embodiment, it is a pitting of skills, tenacity, and plain honest-to-goodness work, with emphasis on work," he concluded.

At Home with the Muse

How literally Nat Horowitz took his alter ego's rhetoric and professional guise is not clear. Whatever the case, he welcomed the opportunity to wash off the tensions of the work routine. Every day during pool season between May and September, he returned home to take a 5 p.m. swim just before dinner, no matter what the weather. He celebrated this ritual in a poem:

> Oddball Horowitz
> Swims in the rain.
> Swimming, old Oddball
> Is feeling no pain.
> Evenballs watch,
> And cluck as they view,
> Poor Old Oddball –
> Nuthin' better to do.
> Primordial rain
> Plasters his face,
> But Oddball keeps goin'
> Won't alter his pace.
> It's an affront to the gentry,
> Who discreetly refrain
> From sinking to swimming,
> In a pluvious rain.

Literary pursuits offered additional release. A ninth grade dropout, Nat made a point of completing the *Sunday New York Times* crossword puzzle each week, although he often asked Dorothy for help on clues that stumped him. Meanwhile, his own portfolio continued to grow.

Fond of narrative turns, Nat completed a short story called "The Pick-up." The plot centered on a married couple who spice up their relationship by pretending they are strangers soliciting sexual favors from each other in shadowy cocktail lounges. Like most of the author's works of the period, the piece remained unpublished. The nonsense verse "Mischa's Concert" was one of Nat's prized projects. The poem lists the distinguished luminaries in the imaginary audience. Among them are "The Pasha of Pisha" and "The Bey of Tunisia," "The Khan of Khantukki" and "The Don of Milwukki," "The King of Letlivia" and "The Prince of Oblivia," "His Nibs from Numonia" and "The Cream of Spumonia," as well as "The Sheik of Chicago" and "The Count of Key Largo."

Several of Nat's musical parodies seemed to have been prepared with Country Club skits in mind although none reached the stage. A take-off from *Oklahoma*'s "The Farmer and the Cowman" contrasted Long Island's North and South Shores and Nassau and Suffolk counties. "The Tribe of Wheatley," in turn, paid homage to Longfellow's "Hiawatha":

> By the shores of Northern Parkway,
> Where the streams of traffic bubble,
> Where the bumpers bump the bumpers,
> Of the Nassaus and the Suffolks,
> Stand the wigwams of the Wheatleys,
> Mighty warriors of North Hempstead.

Dorothy's efforts of the period included "Secret," a brief and intriguing reflection of suburban life that made its way into her personal files but failed to see the light of day:

> I walk and talk a little
> And make the motions of living
> But I have a secret
> Too terrible to tell –
> I am really half-dead, you know,
> And live in the suburbs of Hell.

A lighter treatment of the theme appears in an unpublished short story, "The Little Holiday." Here, a suburban Jewish rebel defies her absent husband's wishes by going out for a Chinese pork dinner and taking in a movie during afternoon hours. Another sketch, "Forty in the Shade," explored a restless woman's fantasies of sexual liberation before she reconciles to her marriage and home life.

September 13, 1958

Everyone took the stage in the Horowitz household. As youngsters, David and Michael had been encouraged to entertain whoever had taken sick with songs, jokes, or impromptu skits. While hosting dinner guests in Roslyn Heights, Nat and Dorothy normally prevailed upon their sons for entertainment. With David at the piano, Michael would present skillful renditions of popular standards such as "I Believe" or even rock 'n' roll hits. As Michael's *Bar-Mitzvah* date approached in 1958, Dorothy suggested that a musical take-off on the pop classic "Bewitched" might make a perfect replacement for the customary reception welcoming speech.

The assignment complemented Nady's Horowitz's penchant for Yiddish-flavored rhyme. Disdainful of the materialism and self-satisfaction he detected in many contemporaries—whom he referred to as "*all-right-niks*"—Nat sought to put on a tasteful but unpretentious *Bar-Mitzvah* celebration in his cherished backyard Arcadia. To accommodate 110 guests at the catered affair, he rented a huge tent for $135, assuring skeptics including his wife that the flaps could open for a refreshing breeze if weather permitted.

Instead, the morning of September 13th brought gale-force winds and torrential rains off the Atlantic. As the family left for the short drive to Temple *Beth Sholom*, a subdued Uncle Mickey volunteered to stay behind to "prepare" for his duties as master of ceremonies. Distraught over the turn of events, he turned to the party's ample stocks of Scotch and Rye. When the festivities began, Mickey's customary talent for crisp oratory gave way to a rambling and barely comprehensible diatribe bemoaning the treachery of a merciless God who had wreaked such havoc on a devout and observant people.

Just when it seemed the event had deteriorated beyond repair, the boys came to the rescue. As David provided accompaniment at the family piano carefully positioned to one side of the tent, Michael took to the microphone to execute a flawless delivery of "Bewitched."

The opening stanza was enough to steal the show:

> A man at last,
> My childhood's past,
> No simpering, whimpering kid at last,
> Bewitched, bothered, and *Bar-Mitzvah-ed* am I!

Choices

Nat's penchant for scripting his boys' performances reflected a desire to raise his progeny within the parameters of Jewish manhood. Along these lines, he urged David to join the Conservative Temple's United Synagogue Youth chapter. After attending the organization's national convention in Buffalo, David addressed Friday evening services with a report on a workshop dealing with the concept of the "Chosen People." He elicited his father's approval on another front when he and a classmate organized a lucrative summer's lawn care business. The duo then joined two friends in a dance band with David serving as piano player. Taken by his son's resourcefulness and entry into the entertainment world, Nat named the group "The Music Men" after the Broadway hit, *The Music Man*.

Dorothy had expectations of her own. When David reached his sophomore year in high school, she began to emphasize the importance of compiling a record of extra-curricular activities before applying to college. David responded by joining the high school newspaper staff, where he published a series of features on career choices. When he became sports editor responsible for a monthly column, Nat named it *Sportniks*—a take-off on Sputnik, the Russian space satellite deployed in 1957. To Dorothy's gratification, the assignment and a satisfactory academic record helped garner David a second-round induction into the National Honor Society.

Michael kept a greater distance from his parents. Yet during the summer of 1959, Nat asked him if he would use the tape recorder and 8 mm movie camera purchased with *Bar-Mitzvah* gifts to produce a color film of a backyard visit from Grandma Becky, then seventy-eight years old. David joined the project with a narrative homage to the family matriarch backed by a soundtrack of a Mozart clarinet concerto. The brothers then moved on to a number of sketches for WMDH—their fantasy radio station. One, taking the form of an ethnic documentary, had Michael playing an elderly "down-home" southern black jazz musician responding to an interviewer's questions. In another series of impromptu "radio" skits, Michael was the straight man as Nat and Dorothy portrayed an East Coast machine politician, a juvenile delinquent, an angry "housewife," and other memorable characters.

Years earlier, Michael had convinced his brother to present a united front against the strong influences of their parents rather than fall victim to "divide and conquer" strategies. This arrangement ensured a certain level of autonomy. At times, Mickey Levine assisted the process. As much as he detested the political apathy and self-indulgence of rock 'n' roll, Mickey could not resist buying a copy of Elvis Presley's first long-playing record for David's fifteenth birthday. Having developed a taste for eighteenth and nineteenth century chamber music, Nat and Dorothy quietly bore these apparent acts of subversion. Even when a friendly "red diaper baby"—the son of former Communists—introduced David to the folk music of Pete Seeger and the Weavers, the couple kept their discomfort with these associations to themselves.

David's grasp at independence became more obvious when he expressed interest in Ohio's progressive Antioch College, a five-year co-educational institution without fraternities, sororities, intercollegiate sports, or compulsory worship. Alternating three-month periods of study with off-campus assignments in the workplace, Antioch boasted a secular, inclusive, and cooperative approach to higher education that appealed to David's growing iconoclasm. Under Dorothy's influence, the official line was that the choice was his. Yet Nat's life-long fixation on the eastern Ivy League remained. Sure enough, he announced that brother Sam, who now worked in the naval yards in Groton, Connecticut, had an "in" at Brown University. This led to a disastrous interview on the Providence campus in which the admissions officer repeatedly interrupted fatherly interruptions to ask what the applicant thought. Furious over the badly botched audition, Nat fumed that the trip was an absolute waste.

The tension over Brown seemed to pass when David received an acceptance letter from Antioch, particularly when a Merit Scholarship through West Chemical guaranteed 20 percent of the yearly $1,000 tuition, the maximum given Nat Harris's income. As David turned eighteen in August 1959, Dorothy escorted him to obtain his Selective Service military registration card and take his driving test. Weeks later, Nat and Dorothy experienced a mixture of pride and regret as they watched David board the New York Central train for Ohio. They had placed an inordinate amount of energy in nurturing their older son and preparing him to face the future. Now that they had, their tightly knit family would never be the same. From now on, they would share David Alan with the rest of the world.

Mrs. Goodfriend

Just as David prepared to leave for college, Dorothy earned her Master's Degree in Education. Two years later, she published a lighthearted poem on her experiences as a substitute teacher in the Bronx in the inaugural edition of *K-Six*, a publication of the New York City School System. By then, she had received her guidance counselor's license.

"The theater, poetry, and music are the outstanding interests in my life," Dorothy reported in her application for an assignment to Corona's P. S. 14.

"Writing gives me great inner satisfaction; also, it is an invaluable aid in teaching and counseling."

"I try to approach children with a sympathetic, as well as a professional point of view," she explained.

Once placed, Dorothy virtually rewrote the job description. The poem "Mrs. Goodfriend Talks to Me" explained what counselors did from a student's point of view:

> Some days at school I feel so bad,
> I feel I want to cry,
> I don't know why I get so bad,
> No matter how I try.
>
> . . . .
>
> One day my teacher said to me,
> "Go to the second floor.
> There is a sign marked 'Guidance Room,'
> Please knock on the door."
>
> . . . .
>
> Once inside the guidance door
> I do not have to worry,
> There I play and talk and draw,
> I am never in a hurry.
>
> Mrs. Goodfriend never scolds
> Her voice is low and nice,
> She listens when she talks to me,
> And gives me great advice.

When meeting groups of students for the first time, Dorothy used "Getting to Know You" from the Rodgers and Hammerstein musical

97

David A. Horowitz

The King and I. Presentations to school assemblies included a parody to "Button up Your Overcoat" entitled "Don't Be an Absentee!" designed to encourage proper health and safety habits. Another program, "Sing, America, Sing," took inspiration from the words of Tom Paine, Woody Guthrie, and Rev. Martin Luther King, Jr.

In spare time, Dorothy composed one of her most ambitious pieces of verse. Although an avowed agnostic, she never had been opposed to employing Biblical prose for polemical purposes. "Genesis Re-Told," written in late 1961, combined a plea for social justice with a prescient view of environmental decay. The subject is an angry God who believes Man has desecrated the Earth with war, killing, malicious falsehoods, and ugliness.

"I AM DONE WITH ALL OF THEE!" He declares.
The Lord then vows to bring forth destruction

hotter than the sun,
deadlier than death,
that no green thing,
no creeping thing,
Shall survive My anger.

When a youth pleads for mercy, he receives instructions to build a spaceship and recruit five others and their wives to escape the devastation. He chooses a doctor to heal the sick, a farmer to grow things, a carpenter to build and not destroy, an artist who "dreams dreams for men," and a teacher of books to instruct the young, the old, the helpless, and ignorant.

Once the chosen ones sail through space, the divine reckoning ensues:

It came to pass that a great heat fell upon the earth,
And lo, the waters dried,
And the green shriveled,
And no creeping thing crept,
And no living thing lived,
And the Lord turned His back on the Earth
That was no longer earth
but....cold....black....stone.

98

Generations

By the early Sixties, Nat Horowitz's literary efforts had assumed an equally reflective tone. John F. Kennedy's assassination produced an ode to Jacqueline. Another poem offered a tribute to Israeli foreign minister Golda Meir as a representative of a revitalized Jewish people. The mellow "Smoke in Autumn," in turn, referred to the author's favorite season:

> Of cracking leaves and crispy air,
> Tinted trees that will soon be bare.
> There is an image that it evokes,
> Of russet fields and farmer's folks,
> A clapboard house with a wisp of lace,
> Curling from a fireplace,
> A horse, a cow,
> A tilted plow ...

When the elderly next-door neighbor passed away, Nat produced "Frank's Tree," a tribute that evoked memories of a spruce that now reached forty feet:

> When I am gone,
> There will be no one
> To know the love
> That Frank had for this tree,
> Which is the lord of the street.

Amid a period of professional and artistic growth, nevertheless, Nat and Dorothy experienced increasing conflict with their sons. Showing remarkable stage presence and a talent for politics, Michael had engineered his election as junior high treasurer with an electrifying campaign speech on student empowerment. Once in high school, he served as campaign organizer and press secretary for the student body president. In Michael's junior year, an inspiring English teacher noticed his writing ability and encouraged him to delve into Symbolist poetry just as friends introduced him to free-form African American jazz. Meanwhile, he starred in a school production of Thornton Wilder's *The Skin of Our Teeth.*

During the Cuban Missile Crisis of October 1962, Michael scripted

99

an original musical extravaganza entitled "The End of Days" based on the life of the Hebrew prophet Isaiah. School authorities vetoed a performance on grounds of separation of church and state. Undeterred, the aspiring artist formed the "Young Lions" production company with a friend and used his movie camera for a series of short art films on the mundane qualities of suburbia and other subjects.

Michael's school teachers heralded his generation as tomorrow's leaders. So emboldened, he and his friends occasionally tested the limits of authority. On one occasion, they hooked up an unauthorized closed circuit radio network to two study halls. Another prank involved the distribution of a leaflet pillorying the Honor Society as an absurd medieval vestige. Outraged by such disrespect for authority, Nat and Dorothy backed the principal's threats of discipline. Only the loyalty of two social science instructors prevented hefty suspensions.

Nat's concerns about his older son differed from his discomfort with Michael's rebellious streak. His anxieties centered on how David would survive the proverbial "world of hard knocks." Having attended two civil rights demonstrations in Washington, D.C. as a high school senior, David joined a team from the Antioch student newspaper to cover Nashville's Negro lunch-counter sit-ins in the spring of 1960. Taken by the imperatives of racial justice, he accepted a college work-study assignment at an inner-city settlement house in Rochester, New York the following year. Ever since David had followed Dorothy's path by declaring himself a Psychology major, Nat had held out the idea of his becoming a psychiatrist—"top man" in the field. Looking past his son's idealism, Nat feared the Rochester job might ultimately lead to a financially and professionally marginal career as a social worker. Worn down by his father's pressure, David agreed to arrange a release from an anticipated second stint at the settlement.

Generational divides also carried over to the world of politics. During a year abroad studying History at Britain's working-class University of Leeds, David absorbed elements of the student radicalism and anti-Americanism following the Cuban Missile Crisis. Letters home now insisted there was no rationale for the murderous impact of war, imperialism, or even national rivalry. Having made the painful transition from socialist pacifism to supporting the military effort to defeat fascism and Nazism after Pearl Harbor, Mickey and Dorothy wanted to know what the proper response to a Hitler would be. David's impatient rejoinder was that their generation saw everything in terms of World

War II. For his part, Nat simply argued that America's faults paled when compared to those of other nations.

During the summer of 1963, Nat and Dorothy took an inaugural trip abroad—including a tour of Israel and the Middle East that included Tel Aviv, East Jerusalem's Hebrew University, the Sea of Galilee, and the Gaza Strip. Stopping over in Rome, they met up with David, fresh from a stint at a British work camp in northern Greece. In a pilgrimage to the city's oldest synagogue, Nat expounded upon the distinct bonds that tied the Jewish people to each other, whatever their native country or language. After the three flew to Paris, extended walks through the city's bustling markets, streets, and alleys permitted father and son to a share an appreciation of Old World culture that seemed to bridge some of their political differences.

Hair

After dropping Psychology for History, David completed college in June 1964. Yet even graduation introduced a generational test of wills. Since Antioch required no caps and gowns, Nat and Dorothy pressed their son to wear one of his father's dark blue suits. In response, David asked twelve women classmates to attest to the fitness of his wardrobe. Not to be undone, Dorothy composed "To the Bright Girls At Antioch":

> Thank you for the affidavit,
> You must think I am a snob
> Because I am so very avid
> That Davey shouldn't be a slob.
>
> Why must all of Antioch frown
> Upon the familiar cap and gown?
>
> For five long years we have waited
> To see our son get "graduated."
>
> Remembering when
>   he
>   was
>   lost
>   in London fogs,

David A. Horowitz

Irish bogs,
Co-op jobs . . . . . .

Oh, I am going to Yellow Springs town,
But my boy won't be in a cap and gown.

Oh, hear me singing those Antioch blues;
Watching patched pants, frayed coat,
and
over-worn
shoes!

Once again, Dorothy and Nat prevailed, although David let them know that his father's baggy pants and oversized suit jacket made him appear completely ludicrous.

Months before Commencement, David had sent several applications to History graduate schools, a decision partly based on the need to maintain a student draft deferment. Nat had suggested he apply to the University of Minnesota, where the son of old family friends taught British history. Although the contact presumably had little effect, the Department admitted him to the program and soon added a first-year teaching assistant's post that came with a discounted tuition for state residents. Meanwhile, David remained on Long Island in search of a summer job to bolster savings. The elusive hunt afforded Nat the opportunity to re-emphasize the relevance of education and a professional career to financial independence. When Bernie Mass belatedly came up with a slot for his nephew on one of his Lower Manhattan construction crews, therefore, Nat felt assured that a season of hard work would provide his eldest some valuable lessons.

Once David moved to Minneapolis in the fall of 1964, he settled into a series of primitive rentals in "an area of transition" near the university. He soon cultivated a small circle of graduate school friends and itinerant locals associated with the emerging counterculture, which had begun to generate the galaxy of anti-materialist values, cooperative ideals, sexual freedom, and alternative spirituality destined to leave a major imprint on American society. David's classes and reading also reinforced an emerging political radicalism increasingly critical of American capitalism and the nation's overseas empire.

Letters home were now far less frequent and left gaping holes in accounts of personal activity. When David spent the summer of 1966 in Roslyn Heights, he had grown out his curly hair and sideburns and identified himself as a Vietnam War opponent and critic of "straight" society. He also had taken up with a liberated woman from an Old Left Jewish family from the North Bronx. Badly misreading his parents' moral compass on one occasion, he invited his friend to spend the night in Roslyn Heights, leading Nat to privately inform him he had disrespected the dignity of their home. David had no choice but to drive his guest back to the Bronx. By the time he returned to Minneapolis for the fall, however, the incident was past history and Nat and Dorothy gifted him their 1961 Chevrolet Impala sedan.

For his part, Michael continued on a steady path to independence. As his younger son weighed options for college in 1963, Nat had reacted to lingering doubts about David's choice of Antioch by suggesting that Michael consider Brandeis University, founded by Jewish donors in 1948. Michael initially dismissed the idea. Yet when he checked out the credentials of radical faculty including Marxists Angela Davis and Herbert Marcuse and the university's superb reputation, he "acceded" to his father's preference. Michael would take Marcuse's advanced class in political science at the end of his second year, followed by a junior year of study in Stockholm that would deepen his interest in radical sociology.

From Sweden, Michael traveled to Leningrad, where he resorted to the official Soviet tourist agency to make contact with remnants of the Levine family. He wound up playing piano for the widow of one of Nat Levine's cousins whose son Leo was a violinist with the Leningrad Philharmonic and often toured the United States. A subsequent letter from the musician's uncle reported the liquidation of two of Nat Levine's sisters in wartime Sluck and the death of a sister-in-law in the German blockade of Leningrad, painful reminders of the evils of Nazism Dorothy had anticipated in her college days.

Once Michael returned to the States, he spent the summer of 1966 as a camp drama counselor in upstate New York, where he directed a group of suburban youngsters in an electrifying version of the musical comedy, *Damn Yankees*. He then moved on to Cambridge to live off-campus for his last year at Brandeis. By now, Michael had grown his hair long, donned dark granny glasses, adopted hipster lingo, and taken on the charismatic persona of a hippie icon. Working with a group of friends, he presided over the production of a counter-cultural publication called *The Living Children*, which anticipated that technological innovation would liberate humans from the tedium of work. Michael also followed media theorist Marshall McLuhan's vision of the world as an electronically connected global village.

In January 1967, both *Books* magazine in New York and the *L.A. Free Press* reprinted Michael's manifesto from the opening pages of *The Living Children*.

"We are the Eternal Children," it proclaimed, "helplessly kicking *Das Kapital* into a pot of paint and calling it the art of love."

"Man's most cosmic desire is to be beautiful—then to eat," it explained.

A new generation would "freak out America," Michael exalted.

"When we've finished," he promised, "this country is going to love itself."

1968

Michael graduated from Brandeis in June. In the fall of 1967 he enrolled in the Political Science Master's Degree program at Manhattan's New School for Social Research. He soon found a seedy but fashionably located apartment in bohemian Chelsea, just north of the West Village. Building on the success of *The Living Children*, he embarked upon a promising counterculture journalism career. Credits included an article in the fashion magazine *Cheetah*, a feature in Boston's *Avatar*, and a portrait of the *Avatar* in the *Village Voice*. In March 1968, *Books* magazine published Michael's "Toward a Positive Politics."

"In our music, in our youth, in our beauty," he proclaimed, "we are tuned to an everlasting harmony."

Michael followed these triumphs with a prestige assignment from *Esquire* for a profile of reclusive rock star Jim Morrison of The Doors.

These accomplishments made little impression on his father. Instead, Nat anguished over his younger son's apparent lack of interest in a steady livelihood, bringing to mind his own Depression futility and brother's Sam's erratic work history. He also remained uncomfortable with Michael's unmanly long hair and hippie demeanor—in his view, an artificial pose that mocked the diligence and sense of responsibility needed for success in the workplace and a healthy family life. Having come late to the pleasures of marriage and then labored so strenuously to provide for his wife and children, Nat cringed at the prospect of both offspring rejecting this most obvious path to personal fulfillment and happiness. To his dismay, neither seemed interested in finding a Jewish life partner or even perpetuating the family line.

The first disappointment along these lines concerned their older son. After passing his PhD written exams during the fall of 1967, David began researching a dissertation on American corporate ideology in the 1920s. That January, he passed on the news that the History Department of Oregon's Portland State College had accepted him for a tenure-track position. In April, he flew back to New York to pursue several archival holdings at Columbia University. As was the custom when the boys returned home, Nat took him to shop for new clothes at his favorite discount outlet and even tried to cajole his son into taking some of his own recent purchases. He also bequeathed his 1967 Impala to David for the return to the Middle West.

Not long after David arrived back in Minneapolis, he called his parents to say that before heading for Oregon at the end of June, he planned to marry Rita, a graduating History student he had known for sixteen months. Dorothy tried to make light of the matter by asking if the prospective bride knew of his intentions, a reference to the single-minded character in *The Graduate* (1967) who continues to insist he will wed the woman who has repeatedly rejected him. In truth, Dorothy had concerns about Nat's willingness to welcome a daughter-in-law whose mother, while of Jewish parentage, was a secular economist at Cornell University, and whose divorced father, an economics professor at Portland State, was a Gentile skeptic.

Intent on placating his parents, David promised to find a rabbi to preside over the exchange of vows under a *Chupeh* (the traditional tent-like ceremonial covering) in the living room of the Minneapolis duplex he shared with a friend. Three weeks before the event, however, Dorothy called to say that Michael, due to be Best Man, would not be able to attend.

The month of June 1968 would present a series of cruel challenges to Michael's dream of a spiritually liberated America. Anxious about a draft board reclassification and devastated by the news that an enraged feminist had seriously wounded avant-garde artist and cultural icon Andy Warhol, Michael put enormous energy into completing the *Esquire* assignment on Jim Morrison. Days later, a Palestinian nationalist assassinated New York Senator and Vietnam War opponent Robert F. Kennedy, the likely contender for the Democratic presidential nomination. With his defenses undermined, Michael experienced an existential crisis of faith that left the author of *The Living Children* with little hope for the nation's future or his place within it.

"If there are no heroes, why live? To watch the trains go by?" he would write in a retrospective three years after the fact.

"Other countries kill," he anguished, "America murders....We spread the rumor that fantasy is possible and then we destroy it. There is nothing more ruthless."

While Mickey stayed behind with Michael in New York, Nat and Dorothy arrived in Minneapolis, where a Reform rabbi presided over the nuptials in the presence of a number of Jewish friends and university associates. At the close of the ceremony, the groom, sporting a fashionable Nehru jacket and a gold medallion, and the bride, outfitted in a long white dress, took part in the traditional glass-breaking ritual to ensure good fortune. Nat and Dorothy did their best to keep up appearances, presenting the newlyweds with a generous check, a blue-flowered set of double-bed sheets, and six packages of Junket pudding mix, David's favorite childhood dessert. Yet the match was not one they had envisioned. Additionally distracted by Michael's emotional state, which confirmed their worst fears about the dangers of the counterculture, they were tense and out of place among the academic and artsy celebrants.

Nat wondered why no one chimed in with a rendition of "The Bride Cuts the Cake."

Following the ceremony, the couple lost little time in flying back to New York.

Schisms

By the fall of 1968, Michael had resolved his draft board difficulties, rebounded from his state of disarray, and resumed studies at the New School. Yet Dorothy faced additional challenges. Even at the height of the "red scare" of the early 1950s, when she discarded several of her Marxist theory books, the former socialist, like Mickey, had reacted critically to the theatrics of Senator Joseph McCarthy and his anti-communist allies. President Lyndon Johnson's escalation of the Vietnam conflict in 1965, in turn, rekindled her youthful antiwar sentiments. In light of public discussion about the "good Germans" who had cushioned themselves against knowledge of Nazi war crimes and atrocities, she sympathized with many Jews and other critics who stressed the need to speak out against any government deploying murderous violence against civilian populations. For Dorothy as well as Mickey, the U.S. presence in Vietnam fit such a category.

When President Johnson dismissed peace activists as "nervous Nellies," therefore, Dorothy came up with the idea of a button stating, "I'm a 'Nervous Nellie—I'm Afraid of War."

SANE (The Committee for a Sane Nuclear Policy) followed up the proposal and sent her several samples of the pin the group mass-produced.

Dorothy's social ideals also extended to racial justice. Like many American Jews, she saw the U.S. Supreme Court's decision against public school segregation in 1954, the successful Montgomery Bus Boycott of 1955-56, and the use of federal troops to integrate Little Rock High School in 1957 as gestures opening society's doors to *all* people. It was easy, therefore, to join Mickey and millions of white liberals in supporting the ideals of the nonviolent and integration-minded civil rights movement. As a teacher and guidance counselor, Dorothy incorporated the human rights rhetoric of Martin Luther King into lesson plans and school assemblies. She even made fun of herself as "a do-no-good liberal who contributed to the NAACP, SCLC, CARE, and all the alphabetical aphorisms for GUILT."

The belligerent posture of Black Power and Black Nationalist advocates of the late-Sixties, however, tested her patience. Following Israel's surprise victory over the combined armies of Egypt, Syria, and Jordan in the Six Day War of 1967, even many secular and casual Jews took pride in the Jewish state. For Dorothy, these sympathies intensified when a segment of African American leaders and many white radicals painted Israel's occupation of Arab territories on the West Bank, Golan Heights, Sinai, and Gaza Strip as a colonial venture.

The split between the organized Jewish community and much of the Left mirrored a growing chasm between white liberals and African Americans. These tensions escalated in the fall of 1968 when a community-controlled school board in a largely black section of Brooklyn abruptly fired many of the district's white and Jewish personnel. African American activists claimed that children of color needed role models in the classroom and a curriculum geared to their needs. In response, the

United Federation of Teachers accused the board of anti-semitism and egregious violations of due process, prompting a citywide strike that lasted two months.

As an original UFT member and chapter organizer, Dorothy fully supported the walkout. Beyond union solidarity, she regretted that the idealism of the civil rights struggle appeared to have degenerated into a belligerent ideology that had spawned ugly reprisals against lifetime educators. A telling indication of Dorothy's growing disenchantment occurred during Christmas break when David and his wife Rita visited from Portland. One night Mickey and Rita's mother came to dinner. When the conversation drifted to the Great Depression, both guests expressed fond memories of a period that they remembered as one of progressive possibility and hope.

Calling to mind Lake Huntington, joblessness, the rise of fascism, the political bankruptcy of Hunter College, and the collapse of socialist dreams, and sobered by the disturbing events of the past year, Dorothy could only recoil in horror.

"It was a terrible time!" she exclaimed of the 1930s.

Not by coincidence, Dorothy soon began accompanying Nat to weekly Temple services.

6

THE PERILS OF SUCCESS

W hatever disappointments Dorothy experienced in the tumult of the late-Sixties, a guidance counselor's vocation offered a vital outlet for her energies. By now, she had transferred to two ethnically mixed schools in Hollis and Bellerose, Queens. Her office featured a toy sign of dry flowers spelling out "LOVE SPOKEN HERE." Yet the assignment was no walk in the park.

Firing Line

Guidance work was "the loneliest, most frustrating job in the educational spectrum," Dorothy observed in "Counselor, What Would You Do?" an article published in 1969 in the journal of the *American School Counselor Association*. The practitioner could never be sure if she was helping children, their parents, or their teachers, she acknowledged. She wondered why there seemed to be more disturbed students every year. Then she recalled the day she told a young girl she could be anything she wanted to become in life, only to learn that, minutes later, the student had gone on a rampage and wrecked the adjacent kindergarten.

"I didn't think she aspired to become a house wrecker," the writer confessed.

Counselors were "constantly on the firing line," Dorothy explained, operating not only by directives but by sheer resourcefulness. The job description ranged from psychologist to attendance officer to health agent to sex education consultant to surrogate parent and babysitter. On one occasion, Dorothy would remember years later, her principal had called her into the office to assist a frightened boy whose fly zipper had caught the top skin of his penis.

Beyond dealing with student problems, as the author noted, the job could require working with creative non-achievers, putting out a Xeroxed student literary magazine, producing a play on civil rights, or organizing student-parent panels on dating, curfews, hairstyles, and homework. As public affairs officers, counselors might find themselves dispensing information on "the Pill, Pot, or Poverty Programs," Dorothy observed. Smoking offered one example. Citing an American Cancer Society prediction that one million of the nation's school children would die of lung cancer before they reached age seventy, the writer argued that public schools had a duty to offer information about tobacco. She suggested having a representative of the local Cancer Society present the facts to students in a non-directive approach devoid of moral posturing.

Having outlined several guidance responsibilities, the article posed a series of questions:

Should a counselor visit a chronic runaway in a temporary youth shelter? Should she volunteer for a faculty committee to evaluate teaching methods?

Should she write guidance columns for the Parent Teachers Association
newsletter and conduct sociodramas for Mothers Clubs?
Should the counselor organize sessions on loaded subjects like the
Dropout rate, the Draft, and Dissent?
Should she offer female students advice on their first menstrual period,
drug use, pregnancy, or rejection from college?

Even though objections could be raised to taking on any of those
tasks, Dorothy replied that each was completely legitimate. If guidance
workers were to "strengthen ego, raise self-concepts, give support, and
inspire our children with renewed confidence," she concluded, they had
to move beyond a textbook definition of the craft.

"We must extend ourselves," her article pleaded,

> to become creative counselors. Since we are living in a changing
> world, then certainly our role will be changing. We cannot afford
> the free choice exercised by a clinic; we can neither pick nor refuse
> our students. When the kids reach out to us, let us be sure that we
> are there to grasp their hands warmly.

Dorothy put her own advice into practice by conducting parental
therapy sessions. At the request of Fay Kanin, who was preparing a
television docudrama on domestic violence, she even brought a number
of Italian and Jewish American women from the Mothers Club to Roslyn
Heights, where she served dinner and led a discussion on the topic. Fay
crafted the group's accounts into "Tell Me Where It Hurts," which won
an Emmy for best dramatic script in 1973.

Despite compiling twenty-six credits beyond the Master's degree,
Dorothy never undertook a PhD dissertation in deference to her
husband's relative lack of schooling. Yet she accepted an appointment
as an adjunct associate professor of graduate education at the C. W. Post
Center of Long Island University in the fall of 1969. Dorothy used the
classroom as a forum for the sort of the questions raised in her article.
Her only setback came when one of Nat's old cronies from the Bronx,
a physical ed teacher in a Brooklyn high school, accused her of taking
herself too seriously when she refused to award his son an undeserving
"A" in one of her classes.

A Far Cry

By 1969, Michael had resumed his counterculture career. That February, the *New York Free Press* published his "Birth of Techno-Technology," a tribute to Marshall McLuhan's theories of modern media and a "retribalizing" planet. Two months later, Cambridge-based *Crawdaddy* printed the profile of Jim Morrison that *Esquire* had declined to publish. Meanwhile, Michael undertook work on "Portrait of the Marxist as an Old Trooper," a humorous treatment of Herbert Marcuse's emerging pop culture status as an advocate of youthful liberation. Once receiving his Political Science Master's degree in the fall, Michael built up savings at home while working at a Long Island bookstore.

For his part, David continued to immerse himself in radical politics and counterculture diversions. Like Michael, his interests reflected his mother's analytic bent and idealism when it came to the critique of American Empire favored by New Left historians of the period. Yet David's appreciation of cooperative cultural values and disdain for thoughtless materialism borrowed important elements of his father's approach as well. Perhaps the two strands explained why he identified with a political and cultural movement that sought to fuse a reconstruction of American capitalism with a liberating social ethic. Whatever the case, he saw no contradiction in publicly speaking out against the Vietnam War as an academic while attending outdoor rock festivals and participating in the bonding pastimes of the alternative culture.

Nat and Dorothy learned of David's emerging lifestyle when he called during the winter of 1970 to report that he and Rita had separated and that he was sharing a flat near the university. Then in June, David informed them of his arrest for disrupting a Portland State classroom during the student strike following President Richard Nixon's expansion of the Vietnam War into Cambodia and the shooting of protesters at Kent State University. Dorothy wondered why David was required to answer for a minor incident while Abbie Hoffman and Jerry Rubin made a joke of the federal prosecution surrounding their antiwar protests during the Democratic National Convention in Chicago two years earlier. In 1971, nevertheless, David finally received his History PhD, formalized his divorce, and emerged from the misdemeanor charge with a year's probation and hundred dollar fine.

At the same time, Nat and Dorothy's hopes for Jewish grandchildren seemed more elusive than ever. David's fascination with the counterculture had led him into a liaison with an alluring young adventurer in a romance that aroused considerable skepticism in Roslyn Heights. When the men's liberation group to which David belonged received coverage in *Life* magazine for its efforts toward overcoming male privilege, Dorothy could not contain herself.

"You are torturing yourself with self-doubts," one of her letters exclaimed. "Why? You are a handsome, young intelligent, sensitive person who is a good teacher at a university. What the hell-else do you want in life? I never promised you—even crabgrass!"

Feminist liberation was "a hoax," Dorothy continued, because nothing could overcome the fact that "the womb apparatus" made women "love objects." Suzanne was such an object, she insisted. "When you get tired of her, there will be another one."

Dorothy's skepticism surfaced in a verse entitled "The Seventies":

> The flower children have faded
> The marijuana-marigolden girls left jaded
> Only the fools and the blind have made it!

Weeks after the *Life* article appeared, David's aging duplex and three adjoining structures went up in smoke in a terrifying fire in the middle of a hot and dry July night. David lost all his possessions, including his recently purchased 1963 Volkswagen bus. Nat and Dorothy immediately sent a thousand dollar check. Within weeks, he and Suzanne found a seemingly fireproof all-rock rental house in Bridal Veil, a hippie enclave thirty miles east in the windswept Columbia River Gorge. By now, David had a full-grown beard and, courtesy of his girlfriend's piercing job, sported a tiny red opal earring in his left lobe. Unthinkingly, he sent a photo home.

"I sat in the temple," Nat confessed in a letter shortly after his sixty-third birthday in September 1971, "and I just couldn't reconcile you—as I know you, with the bearded hairy picture you sent us. You're a far cry from a suburban temple, aren't you Davey?"

The Most of Life

Three months later, Mickey called Portland. On a research trip to New York in 1968, David had visited grandmother Becky's apartment on Popham Avenue to learn about her experiences in Radun, her emigration to London, and the family's early life in New York. After recording her stories by hand in a spiral notebook during a two-hour session, he put away the findings for another day. Within a year of the visit, Becky returned to Popham Avenue from a Miami sojourn to find most of her furniture stolen. Through Mickey's contacts in the Federation of Jewish Philanthropies, she settled into a comfortable suite in a senior facility in the North Bronx, where on one occasion she served tea to Governor Nelson Rockefeller during a campaign stop. Mickey now informed David that Becky, the Horowitz family matriarch, had died peacefully at the age of ninety.

Nat had taken to calling for Becky on Friday afternoon for weekends in Roslyn Heights. He always marveled how his mother would arrive with a pot of a freshly prepared Jewish dinner specialty. An inveterate sentimentalist, Nat took the loss hard, leading Dorothy to gesture to David to comfort his father as everyone gathered in the lobby of the Grand Concourse funeral home. Following the burial at the family plot in Staten Island, Bernie Mass drove his two nephews up to Riverdale through the old Bronx neighborhood. As black and Puerto Rican tenants had replaced fleeing Jewish families in the early Sixties, landlords had neglected the buildings. By mid-decade, heroin addicts had squatted in many of the structures, prompting owners to torch them for the insurance. Bernie pointed to the cyclone fence fronting University Avenue's boarded storefronts.

"Keeps the rats, out," he observed, an ambiguous reference to say the least.

At the Mass apartment, Michael wowed his female cousins with his best counterculture rap. Having published the *Playboy* piece on Marcuse in the spring of 1970, he had gone west to explore journalism possibilities in San Francisco. Now based in Portland, Michael was completing research for a "hippie bible"— an anthology designed to offer excerpts from the world's eclectic spiritual traditions.

Oblivious to David's beard and his brother's long hair, Bernie had a word of advice.

"Just get the most out of your life you can," he said quietly. "You never know."

The Quiet Man

Nat and Dorothy paid their first visit to Oregon during the spring of 1972. A year earlier, they had taken a second trip to Israel with a contingent from the United Federation of Teachers. Both saw the young nation as the ultimate expression of Jewish self-esteem, a pioneer democracy built from the ashes of the Holocaust that offered a potential counterforce to anti-semitism. For Dorothy in particular, Israel offered a vehicle for the idealism and political commitment that many years of disappointment and disillusionment had eroded.

Mickey warned David that his parents had turned quite conservative.

"Offhand, I would say decorate your house with [Moshe] Dayan (not Dylan) busts."

"They keep asking me what they did wrong," Mickey wrote in reference to the absence of grandchildren and a host of perceived hurts.

"I tell them nothing—they have wonderful kids—better than we all deserve."

David arranged for his parents to stay at a rustic set of tidy cabins a mile from his Columbia Gorge home. Admittedly, Dorothy could not help cringing after one of David's cats used the kitchen litter box during an afternoon tea. Yet Nat was completely taken by a stay in Rockaway, a weather-beaten North Coast Oregon resort where he made a fire in the motel's spacious ocean-view suite following a fresh salmon dinner at a local eatery.

"The rain and windswept motel with the grumbling waves" made a lasting impression, he wrote in a subsequent letter of appreciation. "The Oregonian forests, mountains, and shore is even more than what you have been trying to convey to us."

Sitting in on one of David's U.S. history classes, Nat chuckled at the facility with which the bearded professor pilloried prominent figures from Andrew Jackson to Richard Nixon. Half in jest, he said his older son would have made a great rabbi. Dorothy, in contrast, took exception to David's nuanced treatment of Depression president Herbert Hoover.

"I still think he was a bastard," the former Trotskyist confessed, a characterization she attributed to Hoover's refusal to consider federal relief for the nation's needy.

Near the close of 1972, Michael published his "hippie Bible" with a Los Angeles press. *A Freak's Anthology: Golden Hits from Buddha to Kubrick* sought to legitimate the counterculture by placing it within a metaphysical tradition spanning thousands of years. Michael's spiffy introductions strove to make each selection accessible to contemporaries. Visiting New York to promote the book in January, he helped Dorothy usher Nat through surgery to replace an arthritic hip, an early manifestation of a malady that would continue to plague the West representative.

Partly to compensate for these difficulties, Nat Harris had taken to making his rounds with a colleague so that one double-parked the car while the other conducted his sales stops. Extended lunches at Rattner's Jewish vegetarian restaurant on the Lower East Side often spiked up the day. Nevertheless, when Nat turned sixty-five in September 1973, West used the pretext of age and the recent operation to force the twenty-eight-year veteran into retirement.

Nat complained that management wanted to turn over his best commissions to a few rising protégés. Weeks before the dreaded date, he completed a bittersweet reflection that conflated brother Sam's former sales career with his own:

> Sam, Sam the disinfectant man.
> Sold all the gunk to clean up the can.
> Sold all the liquid, sold all the towels.
> And also, the tissue to comfort the bowels.
> Sam, Sam, The quiet man

Undone

Dorothy's short play about mandatory retirement, "65 is Dirty," illustrated the trauma of a character for whom "work was the only thing that really made him happy." Taking into account Nat's difficulty in adjusting to life outside West, she scheduled a sabbatical for the 1974-75 academic year that would serve as a prelude to her own retirement. Dorothy processed her ambivalence about the looming closure of her career in a poem, "To My Three Principals":

> What do you say
> When you say good-bye?
> Do you stifle a sigh?
> Have a good cry?

Do you bite your lip?
Try to be flip?
Do you playfully say,
"It's been fun,
So long, everyone!"

Nat and Dorothy sought to ease the transition to retirement with a trip to California. Renting a car in Los Angeles, they visited Mike and Fay Kanin in Santa Monica, whose world, Nat subsequently reflected, always had been "a millennium from my reach." Moving on to Laguna Hills in Orange County, they toured the gated community at Leisure World where Nat's cousins Mo and Lil Golub had retired. After San Francisco, they headed to Oregon. Their first goal was to see David at the modest Cannon Beach motel Suzanne's mother operated. Nat described the place as "a tumble-down vine-garlanded completely captivating pile of shingle" and pictured the adjacent trailer David shared with Suzanne as a converted chicken coop.

After attending July Fourth fireworks in the old resort of Seaside, whose turn-of-century ambiance pleased Nat to no end, the couple headed for Portland. By now, David had relocated to a 1920s rental house five minutes from downtown. Nat attributed a distinct "Mary Pickford" vintage to what he described as its "Salvation Army Renaissance" furnishings. David had belatedly received academic tenure despite lingering questions over the classroom disruption. Michael, in turn, had secured a waiter's job at a Portland crepe house operated by friends and sold ads and published occasional features on politics and culture for a new local weekly.

"Your mother confides that between your brother (over-developed Consciousness III), and your father (over-developed Consciousness II)," Mickey wrote David in a reference to a recent work contrasting counterculture and corporate values, "she finds it hard to breathe."

By the time Nat and Dorothy visited Oregon in the summer of 1974, Richard Nixon was facing the first stages of impeachment proceedings over obstruction of justice charges in the Watergate Case. Having detailed the scandal in the weekly column he wrote for Portland State's newspaper, David was sure Nixon was on his last legs. Nat appreciated his son's passion. Yet a profound cynicism about power made it difficult for him to believe that the most ruthless politician in the world would ever relinquish office. After the president resigned in early August, David sent him the analysis of Nixon's undoing he published in an Oregon monthly.

A few weeks later, Sam Harris died. After a near-lifetime of financial struggles, Sam had found a position as a marketing liaison with Electric Boat, the prime defense contractor of the Groton, Connecticut shipyards. Nat's melancholy poem, "In Memoriam," applied the sense of loss he felt over expulsion from the workforce to the loss of his brother.

"A monument's a block of stone," he wrote."My memory's in my heart alone."

A note to Garson Kanin explored Nat's sense of dislocation.

"I am a victim of this ruthless disregard to a man's psyche, circumstance, desire, and ability," he confessed. "The term 'mandatory retirement' makes me spit."

Another verse, "Towards Evening," expressed similar feelings of regret:

> The leaves curl inwards,
> Wrinkling day by day,
> Withdrawing into themselves...
> The aggressive world is a pushing threat...
> . . . .
> I wanted to touch the skies,
> I wanted recognition—
> For qualities never proven?
> Never heeded? Or perhaps, non existent.

Seeking to prod her husband out of his funk, Dorothy encouraged him to produce an account of the summer's adventure. The title, "I Tripped Over the West," referred to both his former employer and the journey itself. Much of the work reflected the light-hearted approach Nat liked to bring to writing. In a gift shop in the California Danish community of Solvang, he imagines a telepathic message from a ceramic duck asking him to take it home. Other passages describe a friendly encounter with a bearded Berkeley patriarch, a mountain rock formation he christens "Cary Granite," a bond with a California hippie over the beauty of the Redwoods, and swimming alone at 5 a.m. in the indoor pool of an inn at Yosemite National Park. A description of a series of experiences with restroom facilities entitled "Johns I Have Known" follows.

A particularly moving segment of the account centered on the Grand Canyon, which Nat had not seen since 1936. He describes the wonder as "the necklace of America, the brooch on its bosom, the diamonds on its fingers."

'I'm showing this to you,' he hears a voice saying, 'this is a Covenant between thee and Me, a sign between us, because you love my world.'

The most poignant portions of the text deal with the traumas of retirement. As the author describes preparation for bed one night, he recalls a lifelong ritual:

> I sit in my stockinged feet and scrutinize my shoes. We've been together an awful lot, old buddies.... Thanks, ped pals, for lugging me around on your down-trodden heels.

At Leisure World, cousin Mo shows off Olympic-sized heated pools with adjoining hydrobaths, whirlpools, and Jacuzzis and a workshop for every imaginable hobby. This only leads to a series of bittersweet musings.

"I was a top man in my field but through the kindly intervention of the ruling echelon of my solicitous company," the author explains with more than a hint of sarcasm, "I was relieved of the rigors of the skills I knew best."

Now, he admits, as days get more precious, he is "visualizing fall and winter days without the programming of fifty-three years of hard labor."

"Do you just turn off habits of a life as you would a water faucet?" he asks.

"Dorothy, darling, hold my hand," he implores:

> Help me over the hump, sweetheart. I'm scared stiff. My mother taught me to be honest, to be good, to raise a family, to treasure your wife, to work hard, hard, hard! Mom, I've done it all, am I now undone?

Great Expectations

Mike Kanin enjoyed the manuscript. "It simply bears out my contention all along that you have a fine natural talent for writing," his one-time collaborator enthused.

Mike now proposed a complete program of intensive writing, reading, study, research, and travel to nourish the artistic growth and self-examination creative work required. For his part, David published the passage on retirement in his Portland State column in February.

Unlike David and Dorothy, Mickey had little sympathy for his brother-in-law's angst.

"I can't believe he can't find something worthwhile to do where the rewards will not be West commissions but a satisfaction of having helped someone—something," Mickey complained. By this time, nevertheless, Nat and Dorothy had moved on. They already had collaborated on a proposed television script for *All in the Family*, which Mike Kanin registered with the Writers Guild and sent on to producer Norman Lear. The episode centered on Archie Bunker's hatred of birthdays and fear of advancing age. Yet a personal note from Lear contended that the authors failed to understand the main character and lacked an "ear" for Archie's speech.

Seeking to keep Nat engaged, Dorothy convinced him to compile a personal memoir.

"She has noted down for me a whole outline of what I had always believed was a quite passive, fairly un-dramatic life," Nat marveled in a letter to Portland. He now accepted the idea that "every life ever having been lived is well worth writing about."

As David completed his final term of teaching before starting a sabbatical leave, Nat sought to interest him in a visiting professorship in Jerusalem or Tel Aviv:

> Why don't you snoop around your world of academia and come up with a proposition to Israel.... You'll love those Jews, Dave, they are a remarkable people. When I think of your enthusiasm for people and I transpose you into the ancient world of deserts and mountains, I can nearly see a shepherd's crook in your arm.

Nat described Israel as a new nation in an old land. He was sure that the excitement of building a new society would capture his son's imagination. Like his parents, however, David tended to go his own way. As a political progressive, he continued to be uneasy about Jewish relations with the Palestinian and Arab world. In the end, he decided to spend the summer and fall of 1975 in Washington, D.C. reporting for two Portland publications on the Senate's inquiry into the U.S. intelligence community. Meanwhile, Nat and Dorothy spent a month touring Israel.

Two months after their return from the Middle East, the couple hosted a visit from David as Congress broke for the Christmas holidays. By now, Nat had completed his memoir. *The Autobiography of Nady Horowitz: The Young Years* offered a wealth of detail covering the author's childhood and upbringing, his adventures in the workforce, the workers compensation racket, his trip to Los Angeles and creative writing efforts, his courtship of Dorothy, and finally, their wedding. David agreed to send out copies to several New York publishers, although the manuscript's sentimentality and his father's lack of stature elicited polite rejections at best. Nat, however, was more concerned with his son's prospects.

Months earlier, he had praised David's newspaper and magazine pieces for their clarity.

"It's time for you to stop cocking around," he advised, "and embark on a solid project."

For once, David responded to his father's advice when he accepted an offer from freelance academic Peter Carroll to serve as a co-author on a twentieth century U.S. history textbook. Meanwhile, Dorothy continued to encourage her husband's creative writing. He described these efforts in "More Time," a poem that has a solicitous spouse gently prompting her partner to finish a poem. In another verse, "I Came Back So Soon," the author remembers that his beloved asked him to kiss her before he left.

Despite an enormous ability to minister to her husband's needs, Dorothy had her limits. During the summer of 1976, she nursed Mickey in Roslyn Heights when he suffered a minor stroke following gallbladder surgery. Just at that time, Michael returned home at loose ends. With prospects for freelance journalism drying up, he had qualified for a federal Comprehensive Employment and Training Act (CETA) grant in 1975 and taken a position as a fundraiser for a Portland social agency serving alternative street youth. When the money ran out, however, he despaired about his next move in a stagnant economy.

Feeling overburdened, Dorothy asked David for help. By then, however, he was on a two-month break at a beach resort halfway down Mexico's Pacific Coast. Fortunately, by the time he returned to Long Island, Mickey had recovered and Michael was looking forward to a position in the fall as faculty advisor to an Urban Studies monthly at Portland State. In September, the boys returned to Oregon together where they planned to share David's rental house while Michael split his time between the university and a new downtown weekly.

Worldly Vistas

With both sons situated in the Pacific Northwest, the couple undertook a visit to Spain and Portugal in the winter of 1977 as Dorothy's sixtieth birthday approached. The excursion stimulated an outpouring of poetry. As usual, Nat found much to inspire his sense of humor.

"Forgive, forgive, your indulgence pray," he confessed in "Stranger in a Strange Land," "Today I peed in the bidet!"

Other poems described toothpaste-savouring ants in the hotel sink, unnumbered rooms, overdue dinners, sudden electric blackouts, and 'beachfront' accommodations facing concrete walls. "Birthday in Granada," however, offered a tender response to Dorothy's milestone:

> Ssh, my sweetest little lady,
> Rest your head upon my chest,
> That I may keep you closely pressed.
> Come, my love, my moon, my star,
> That I may prove how young we are.

"The Rocks of the Algarve," returned to Nat's fascination with Nature in the raw:

> The wind comes with time-tempered chisel,
> And chips at the sandstone of the Algarve.
> The spray leaves rivulets of tears
> On the carvings of the Algarve,
> Then the sun, soothing and warming,
> . . . .
> Bakes them into eternity.

Dorothy offered her own homage to the scene:

> But oh, to be a poet
> To catch the mood of the Algarve
> In rhyme and meter.
> The sea would change from drizzle, damp mist
> To dazzling sunlight burning the fog.
> My picture – my music – my poem
> Would remember the moment of loveliness.

Once the couple returned from Europe, they began planning a return to Israel. Nat's enthusiasm carried over into a letter to Michael, whose modest income still depended upon the post at the university and occasional stories in the local press.

"There is no work in the world that is demeaning except dishonest or immoral pursuits," Nat acknowledged. "But, sonny boy, your Bronx Momma and Papa had other visions for their exceptionally bright children."

His answer was a period of work in Israel to open up new horizons —"a year of doing the things you went to college for and got a Master's degree."

To emphasize the point, Nat offered to subsidize his son's travel expenses. Yet Michael had his own agenda. Intent on improving his position in the job market, he entered Portland State's Urban Studies PhD program in the fall of 1977, where he planned to undertake a dissertation on the strategic vulnerabilities of the alternative youth center he had recently served. Meanwhile, he took the role of adviser to a group of hippies fighting the gentrification of their Portland neighborhood in Penny Allen's independent film, *Property* (1978).

Just after Michael enrolled at Portland State, Nat and Dorothy joined an American Jewish Committee trip to Turkey, Greece, and Israel. Much of their interest focused on Jerusalem, the location of the *Yad Vashem* Holocaust Museum and Hebrew University. At the university synagogue, the couple met Ruth and Saayah Maximon, two Brooklyn natives laying the groundwork for *aliya*—permanent immigration to the Jewish state. As the foursome became fast friends, the Maximons revealed that their son Jonathan, an Israeli Army veteran, had founded the nation's first reform *kibbutz* in the Negev desert, a half-mile from the Jordanian border.

Separate Ways

The encounter with Ruth and Saayah and their friends' pride in their son helps to explain the dismay that accompanied the news that David was about to enter a second marriage. Back in June, he had informed his parents he was about to set up housekeeping in Southeast Portland with the new woman in his life. "Charmaine" was a twice-divorced former Roman Catholic with three children between the ages of twelve and sixteen. She earned a living conducting poetry workshops in the public schools and waiting on tables for a downtown tavern that attracted alternative poets and musicians. To raise the down payment for the five-bedroom residence the two had in mind, David asked his parents for a bridge loan until Charmaine's own house sold.

The request caught Nat and Dorothy off guard. Based on a combined 130 years of experience, Dorothy responded in a letter, it seemed foolish to buy an older home until you had unloaded the other. Besides, she feared the move might distract David from his textbook project. Despite her son's avowed aversion to the entanglements of a family, she warned, he would be assuming the obligations of a mortgage, a house, another person, and three teenagers.

The crux of the matter, however, concerned Jewish grandchildren.

"I just feel sad for the things we hoped for in life," explained Dorothy, "—and I see now that it becomes more apparent that we'll never have them."

If she and Nat advanced the money, Dorothy reasoned, they would be a party to something they saw as a drastic mistake. On the other hand, they never wanted their son to feel let down when he needed financial help. To resolve the dilemma, the couple sent a $850 gift.

Once Nat and Dorothy returned from Israel in November, David announced he and Charmaine were to be married the following month. He assured his parents that the ceremony would take place in the study, not the sanctuary, of a Portland Unitarian church with absolutely no references to Christianity. Yet these gestures did not address the heart of the problem.

"Your letter left us numb, saddenly aware of the piled up years," Nat responded:

It is not easy to accept the abortion of a family line. And our sadness is not for us alone, but for you, little Davey, my son, denying yourself the unutterable joy of a child of your own, and what seems to me, the complete denial of your Jewish tradition, which has the enrichment of thousands of years of development. I am sad that my influence has not had the strength to stand up against others.

"The Lord alone knows how many years are left for me," he concluded,

but I had hoped that the fruit of years of sweat, heartache, and knocking at doors could have been used to perpetuate our togetherness – your children – our children.... We love you, Davey, and because we love you so much, we cry...
Take care of yourself, Pop.

Gone West

With David's seeming rejection of his family heritage and Michael appearing to flounder on the other side of the continent, the late-Seventies ushered in a period of painful reflection. Nat's poem, "I Remember You My Sons," captured the mood:

> Why did I cry
> When the snow began to fall?
>
> The glinting flakes
> Boxed the seams
> Of my red brick patio,
>
> and the sycamore
> in quiet acquiescence took
> the snuggling snow
> into its arms,
> and cradled it ...
>
> Her leaves had left her
> Many days ago.
>
> I cried because
> My arms are empty.

Nat and Dorothy would not see their older son or meet Charmaine until Michael brought them together in August 1980 for a reconciliation meeting in Roslyn Heights. Charmaine offered to convert to Judaism. Yet weeks later, David concluded he had not succeeded in co-parenting three troubled teenagers in a dysfunctional household or gained the trust of an emotionally fragile spouse. He now moved into the basement of the rental house since Michael had taken over the second bedroom for his dissertation notes, and announced he intended to seek a divorce.

If his son needed financial assistance, a euphoric Nat responded, "ask us for it. If you have problems, let us in on it."

A week later, Dorothy sent a thousand dollar check and offered to pay a monthly stipend to help with David's temporary spousal support payments.

"We are thankful that you have emerged into the open air," Nat exulted. "There are plenty of burdens in living without looking for them."

In November 1980, Nat and Dorothy voted for Independent candidate John Anderson to protest President Jimmy Carter's failure to denounce a UN resolution that proposed to divide West and East Jerusalem between the Israelis and Palestinians. Days later, they joined their rabbi and a Temple contingent on a "Great Jerusalem Pilgrimage" organized by the American Jewish Congress to demonstrate the importance of the Holy City to world Jewry. They even received a private briefing from Israeli Prime Minister Menachem Begin, who embraced the rabbi as an old friend. Nat was adamant that a unified Jerusalem remain under Israeli rule. At the same time, he loved to walk through the city's Arab markets and barter with the vendors over *falafel* and other delicacies. He and Dorothy also relished the tour's visit to Cairo, a result of the normalization of relations between Egypt and Israel that President Carter had brokered at Camp David.

Upon returning to Roslyn Heights, Nat and Dorothy began reassessing their future in the house they had occupied for nearly twenty-five years. There was much to love about the Country Club Homes. Nat felt such an attachment to the place that when Dorothy pressed to have the lower branches of the front shrubs trimmed to let in more light, he reacted in panic.

"It was like cutting my own limbs," he confessed in a letter to David. "Changes get more and more difficult for me to take as the years are added to my life."

Both Nat and Dorothy loved to take overnight jaunts to remote Montauk Point on Long Island's eastern end, a site where Nat's favorite poet, John Hall Wheelock, had depicted "the high lonely stars." Then there were short trips to the Jones Beach Marina, where they would wait for the fleet to dock at 3 p.m., buy fresh cleaned fish for three or four dollars, and grill them that evening for intimate dinners by the fireplace. Nat also basked in the ritual of walking to the Temple on Saturday mornings and admiring the tastefulness of the simple but well-designed single-story brick structure located atop a hillside slope. Sitting in the natural wood interior of the sanctuary, he experienced an inordinate sense of peace when following the rabbi's erudite sermons or losing himself in the comforting harmonies of the professionally trained choir.

As pensioned retirees with substantial savings in certificates of deposit, the couple had benefited from the rising interest returns associated with the oil price hikes and inflation of the late-Seventies. The resulting financial security enabled them to escape harsh Northeast winters and the icy streets that confounded Nat's arthritic limbs. Yet even when they were away in balmy Florida, the Caribbean, Mexico, or Hawaii, heating and house maintenance costs were becoming prohibitive. On more than one occasion, the pipes of the radiant heating system had frozen, leading to steep repair bills. Nat and Dorothy also noted how many friends were retiring to Florida, resulting in a dramatic fall-off in their circle of acquaintances. Finally, both David and Michael were on the West Coast, nearly three thousand miles away.

Contemplating these considerations as the winter of 1981 approached, they opted to rent an apartment for the season at Leisure World with an eye toward a possible move to southern California. The reconnaissance mission garnered unexpected dividends when they discovered a newly built section of unattached two-bedroom condominiums with two full bathrooms in Casta del Sol, a gated senior community in Mission Viejo within ten miles of Laguna Hills. Before they could proceed, however, they needed to sell their own home, an enormous challenge amid skyrocketing mortgage rates and the depressed economy of the early 1980s.

Operating without a real estate agent, Nat became physically ill when prospective buyers dismissed the attractions of his cherished refuge. Finally, the house sold at a substantial discount at the end of spring. Even the reduced price, however, was nearly six times the original cost and comfortably more than a replacement at Casta del Sol would require.

After losing a bid on a property on the melodious sounding Espinoza Drive, located at the end of a quiet cul de sac with a view of the surrounding hills, Nat and Dorothy had a stroke of luck when the original buyer backed out. By August, they were ready to take possession.

Ever the sentimentalist, Nat grieved over leaving the only home he had ever owned:

> My house stands clenched, it's tautly still,
> A quivering drape at a window sill.
>
> The faucet drips a crystal tear,
> The hearth is cold, charred and black,
> The warmth I knew will not be back.
>
> . . . .
> They have their ways to say goodbye,
> But to a house, not so I.
> No, not so I.

Once the moving van pulled out of the driveway, Nat and Dorothy packed their Chrysler sedan with a few essentials and began the cross-country journey. In September, friends and relatives received a Jewish New Year's postcard with a drawing of two covered wagons with the word "California" scrawled on their outer shells.

Inside, the couple's new address appeared with a greeting.

"Gone West!" it proclaimed.

7

GOLDEN RAYS

Southern California's mix of mountains, desert, sun, and sea and the cheerful pastel stucco of its Mediterranean architecture brought back memories of Israel. Freed from the burdens of home maintenance and eastern winters, financially bolstered by high saving rates, and close to both sons on the West Coast, Nat and Dorothy felt they were beginning a new life. Like the Roslyn Country Club, Casta del Sol featured a huge community swimming pool although this one was heated for all-year use, a distinct advantage given Nat's increasing arthritic and circulatory problems. A modern Conservative synagogue, recently purchased from a disbanded Baptist Church, offered a welcome amenity a five-minute drive away.

The Pier

Beyond the opportunity to sample the natural wonders of the California landscape, retirement in Mission Viejo presented new opportunities for creative writing. Taking inspiration from Depression lyricist and wit Yip Harburg and the romantic verse of John Hall Wheelock, Nat devoted a great deal of time to writing poetry. Sent several samples, Mike Kanin continued to lobby for more self-criticism, depth, and universality. "The Pier," a meditation on the restorative power of the ocean inspired by visits to nearby Dana Point, was one response:

> As I enter the pier
> A cloud clasps a hand over the sun
> And the calm is undone.
> The sea serene
> Now sullen green
> Snarls and bares its gums,
> Hissing and roaring
> It hammers the beach
> And spatters like fat in a pan.
> Head in collar
> Fists in pockets
> I crawl further into myself.

Another poem, "Intrusion," used the sea's power as a point of comparison:

> Ocean, be calm, my trespass is humble,
> Your breath on my face is all that I seek,
> I wander your sands and in homage I stumble,
> You are the might, I am the weak.

Three reflections on aging took their place in the portfolio. The first, "Senior Whirl," offered a lighthearted approach to the leisure life:

> Experts say for me to thrive,
> Past the age of sixty-five,
> Busy, busy, I must keep,
> And not devote my days to sleep.

> Ride a bike, climb a hill,
> Careful, though, to take my pill,
> Quite surprising, exercising,
> Keeps the pressure from rising.
> Katatski, Hora, Hoe-Down, Hustle,
> Damn arthritis! Move a muscle!
> Golf and tennis, Bridge, Backgammon,
> Discounted meals of franks and salmon!
>
> Courses, courses, how they make 'em!
> I should only live to take 'em!

The second, "Metallurgy," contemplated mortality:

> My golden years are topped with silver,
> And bottomed with the weight of lead,
> The ore-rich veins that served my liver,
> Need alloys now to keep them fed.
>
> Bonanzas were my lodes of iron,
> That steeled my springs through thick and t'in,
> I panned my streams, a youthful lion,
> With brassy cheek and coppered skin.
> My golden bones are mutely creaking,
> My golden mines are flaked with rust,
> Thus Father Time must do his wreaking,
> And Mother Earth must claim her dust.

"Choice" offered a retrospective dose of realism:

> If once again
> I had a choice
> Of roads unknown,
> I'd ask for this:
> A sturdy soul ...
> And heels of steel
> To bear the wear

A Yiddish Heart

Seeking to expand his horizons, Nat took a college course in TV writing. He even tried to interest an agent in a soap opera segment that depicted a beautiful woman's fear of growing old. Then he sent *Playboy* a satirical piece entitled "Sex Writing Is Easy."

"I have observed that the most widely known and publicized novels," Nat's alter ego declared, "have to do with violence and sex. And so that's what I'll have to write…"

The would-be author proposes a story in which a married man poisons his dying wife so he can wed a young model he has bumped into at Bloomingdale's Department Store. Following the ceremony, his nineteen-year-old son entertains designs on his stepmother, who has her own thoughts about ravaging the boy. This leads the writer to speculate that he might end the tale with a triple suicide.

"I don't know," he concludes. "I'll come back to it later. One thing I know, sex writing comes easy for me."

Playboy responded with an appreciative letter but begged off publication. Then, as national unemployment reached 9.7 percent in December 1982, Nat dispatched a segment of his Depression poem, "The Buyer Said a Merry Christmas," to the *L.A. Times*. The newspaper's publication of the verse coincided with Mike Kanin's suggestion that Nat submit portions of his memoir to the English-language edition of the New York-based Jewish monthly, *The Forward*.

Back in 1978, the magazine had published "A Christmas Story," Nat's sketch about an elderly Jewish shopkeeper who takes a part-time job as Santa Claus during slack season. He now sent *The Forward* an autobiographical segment entitled "I Remember Soho" that described his dropping out of high school to work as a common laborer in Lower Manhattan. The editors also ran another memoir excerpt, "The Bosses Should Boin'," which detailed the brawl with company thugs who had beaten Barnett during Nat's workers compensation days.

Returning to fiction, Nat produced "Grandpa Birnbaum"—a sketch of a Jewish widower whose son, like David, has informed his father that having children is just "not in the cards." The piece did not make it into print. Over the next two years, however, *The Forward* published two other stories. "Louie Abramson Died" centered on three elderly Jews who frequent a Lower East Side park bench, where they taunt each other with loving Yiddish insults and fabrications. "A Visit from My Father," in contrast, pursued a vaguely autobiographical theme.

The first-person story describes the appearance of the narrator's long-deceased father on his suburban patio. As the writer shows off his stylish ranch house, the older man takes note of the light penetrating the floor-to-ceiling Thermopane windows, a stark contrast to the obstructed daylight of the old Bronx tenements. Yet he wonders why his son keeps no *tybelekh* [pigeons] on the roof, as so many of his neighbors once had done.

> "*Nu, Nutteleh*, you called me," the visitor says.
> "*Tsurris* [trouble], Pop, *tsurris*," the narrator answers.
> "*Tsurris*," the apparition shrugs. "*Nu*, who lives without *tsurris*."
> "It's better than not life, no?—not living, not nothing," he counsels.
> "Life comes sometimes like sweet cream, a measure joy, a quarter maybe sweat, work."

The narrator then reports that after tossing aside her college degree, his daughter had joined a "Jews for Jesus" commune in the Ozarks before moving on to an Indian guru's retreat in Colorado. Meanwhile, his professor son, three thousand miles away on the West Coast, had married a twice-divorced Gentile woman with a troubled fourteen-year-old son.

"This is what the colleges did for him?" the visitor responds. "Maybe a Yeshiva might have been better."

As he prepares to leave, the caller gathers his thoughts:

> Grandchildren you ain't got? You're complaining about troubles you got now without grandchildren, no? ... You live in a palace with glass walls and green grass, that you don't have pigeons you have only yourself to blame ... If you wouldn't have troubles would you know what happiness is?

With the relationship with *The Forward* intact, the magazine ran four of Nat's older poems—"One Tongue," "Twilight in Jerusalem," "Dear Momma Golda," and "Geneshe"—the last a tribute to the selfless courage with which Becky's mother faced death. The focus on Jewish themes coincided with Nat's regular attendance at Friday night services and Hebrew and Bible classes, to which Dorothy accompanied him. He even took advantage of the Temple's Brotherhood Week celebration to recycle "Four Chaplains," an older poem that described how a quartet of clergy from the Roman Catholic, Protestant, and Jewish faiths had given their lifebelts to four enlisted men when their transport sank in the North Atlantic during World War II.

Above all, the Temple affiliation offered the chance for Nat to return to his first love through the Yiddish cultural club or *"Vinkle"* he took a lead in organizing. Once again addressed as Nady, he now staged his own translations of Mother Goose rhymes, Dorothy Parker's poetry, and songs like the classic 1890s ballad, "After the Ball." One of his creations was a bilingual adaptation of "Snow White and the Seven Dwarfs." Here, the shrewish queen asks the mirror on the wall to name the fairest on Laguna Mall. Since it is *Yom Kippur* and lying is a sin, the mirror must acknowledge that it is "Little Snow White." Mad with envy, the queen burns the *kugel*, spoils the *strudel*, and lets her *blintzes* get greasy before dispatching the ritual kosher slaughterer to do away with her rival, leading Snow White to flee to the cottage of the Seven Dwarfs.

"Heigh, ho, Heigh ho," she hears them singing as they return home:

> It's home from *shul* we come.
> We swayed and prayed
> And *brukhes* [prayers] made,
> Heigh, ho, *Umain* [Amen].

Seeking a safe refuge, Snow White promises to make herself of use. "I'll cook, I'll clean, I'll keep house for you," she pleads. "I keep *milkhik* [dairy] and *flaishik* [meat], and I make a mean *lukshen* pudding."

In the end, the queen's effort to poison Snow White with tainted *latke* potato cakes comes to naught when "Prince Charmin" arrives to rescue her and make her his bride.

The Mission Viejo Jewish community had never come across anyone with the ability to convert *Yiddishkeit* into captivating entertainment. For a Jewish New Year greeting in 1982, Vinkle member Teddi Lipton offered a fitting tribute to the group's muse. Nady reminded her of all the men her father brought home from *shul* on *Shabbes* for a little *Schnapps*, a glass of tea, homemade pickled herring, *gefillte* fish, *chaleh*, and sponge cake, she recalled. The *Vinkle's* inspiration was a beautiful man "with a sensitive soul and a Yiddish heart."

Our Young and Old

Nady had been playing with lowbrow comedy for some sixty years. Yet he also demonstrated an inordinate commitment to high-minded Jewish idealism and ethical values. This became clear in the rousing finale of the Yiddish club's first presentation, "Wrinkles from the Vinkle," when Nat had the entire audience join a tribute to Jewish self-esteem, democratic values, and solidarity with Israel by singing his adaptation of "America the Beautiful":

> How beautiful to be a Jew
> Endowed with Jewish pride,
> Jerusalem our citadel,
> Our city unified.
> Oh, Is-ra-el, A-mer-ica!
> God shed His grace on thee,
> With sisterhood and brotherhood,
> And hands across the sea.
>
> Oh, Is-ra-el, our Father's dream
> Borne throughout the years.
> Thine alabaster cities gleam,
> Attained through vales of tears,
> Oh, Is-ra-el, A-mer-ica!
> In friendship stand aligned,
> And both imbued with brotherhood,
> And peace for all Mankind.

Never one to make a show of religiosity, Nat nevertheless revered the learned tone of the Scriptures, the rabbinical commentary it generated, and the peace of quiet meditation. As the synagogue prepared a new cabinet for its Torah scrolls, he composed "Dedication of the Ark," a devotional poem whose final line and Temple motto came from a call by Moses in *Exodus*:

> In quavering tones the old *Torah* spoke, its parchment cracked and
>   patched,
> "You didn't have to do this, this thing that you have done,
> I am old and the warmth of your love
> Is gift enough for me, my son."

135

. . . .
"Only because of thee," I said, "this shrine will shine,
Reflecting the light that within it lies."

And thus it shall be, as we have always told,
We will go with our young and with our old.

Moved by its sentiments, the congregation president had the poem mounted as a permanent fixture on the sanctuary wall.

My *Feh* Lady

Nat coupled a feel for raucous comedy and admiration of Jewish tradition in his most ambitious parody, a take-off on *My Fair Lady* intended as a Temple fundraiser. Originally called "My Fair *Shiksa*," the title turned into "My *Feh* Lady" when the synagogue's progressive young rabbi viewed the colloquial reference to a Gentile woman as demeaning. For Nat, the term "*shiksa*" was a lighthearted and harmless component of Jewish folklore. Besides, he insisted that his script treated the virtuous Eliza with complete respect and dignity.

Rendered in English with a few Yiddish expressions thrown in for emphasis, Nat's lyrics mirrored the exact meter and cadence of the Broadway production, an accomplishment he facilitated by having David guide him through the original sheet music.

The action begins with a take-off of "Why Can't the English?" as Rabbi Jonah Finkle and theologian Pashe Pincleman discuss the decline of the Yiddish language in modern day life and the Saddleback Mountain community of Mission Viejo:

Why can't our *lontzlite* [countrymen] teach our children how to speak?
Because we are chosen must they think that we are unique?
A *lontzmon*'s way of speaking absolutely classifies him,
Pronouncing *brait* instead of *broit* – other Yiddish folk despise him.
One common tongue I'm afraid we'll never get,
Oh, why can't our brethren learn to set
A good example to people whose Yiddish is painful to the ears
Litvaks or *Glitzyonner* leave you close to tears.
In Saddleback, they haven't used it for years!

Things proceed from there when Eliza O'Doul returns from six months of study and work at an Israeli *kibbutz* and seeks a mentor to facilitate a conversion to Judaism.

"Let a *kibbutz* in your life and your reeling brain goes free," she sings to the tune of "I'm an Ordinary Man."

"The *kibbutzniks* and the *Sabras* and the Hebrew abacadabras I adore!"

The prospect of taking on a Gentile convert leads the Rabbi to his version of the song:

> I'm an ordinary Jew
> Who desires nothing more
> Than just the ordinary chance
> To serve the Lord I love.
>
> . . . .
> But let a *shiksa* in your life
> And you are absolutely through!
> Will she learn to salt and *vaik*,
> And how to kosher make?
> A *bristle* that is salted
> Is not kosher with a malted.
> It's not clever to let a shiksa in your life.
>
> I think that I would much rather
> Be a martyr on *Masada*
> Then to ever let a *shiksa* in my life!

Once the rabbi agrees to mentor Eliza, she triumphs in mastering the Yiddish phrase, "*De Khrrain iz rane, farshimelt nisht de tzain*" [the horseradish is pure—does not discolor teeth], a triumph the duo marks by singing a rousing version of "The Rain in Spain." By now, the student has fallen in love with her teacher, as Eliza sings to the tune of "Wouldn't It Be Lovely":

> All I want is for him to look
> Up at me from his *Pentateuch*.
> Lay down his Holy Book,
> Oh, wouldn't it be lovely!
>
> . . . .
> The Bible tells us that forsooth,
> A *shiksa* too, Naomi's Ruth.

Rabbi Finkle has similar feelings toward his charge, as he reveals in an adaptation of "I've Grown Accustomed to Her Face:"

> I was serenely unaffected
> A peaceful, righteous Jew,
> But studying the *Torah*
> Is now hard to do.

As the two agree to marry once the conversion is complete, Eliza's Irish father announces his intention to follow suit to the tune of "With a Little Bit of Luck":

> The Lord alone shows no man no favors,
> Be he from Orange or from County Cork,
> The Lord he shows no man no favors – but –
> With a little bit of luck
> With a little bit of luck
> He's a Jewish mayor of New York!

O'Doul then celebrates the match to the tune of "Get Me to the Church on Time":

> I'm getting Jewish in the morning,
> *Ov vey*, I've butterflies inside.
> Oh my, it's scary, I can't say Hail Mary.
> So get me to the *shul*, get me to the *shul* on time.
>
> I'm getting Yiddish in the mornin'
> Lord knows, am I doin' right?
> *Knishes* concern me,
> *Blintzes* heartburn me,
> Get me to the *shul*,
> For Gawd's sake, get me to the *shul* on *tzite*!

When Eliza passes the conversion test, Pincleman offers a version of "You Did It":

> She is now a *shrester* [sister]
> To Golda and Queen Esther
> The rabbis who tested
> Beamed at her and blessed her.

138

At that point, the chorus joins in:

> Congratulations, Rabbi Finkle,
> Sing a psalm and blest be you.
> Everything you strove for, it now belongs to you.
> This evening, sir, she did it!
> She did it! She did it!
> We thought she'd be erratic,
> But she was so emphatic,
> And we all knew she did it!

Twilight Village

Like Nat, Dorothy responded to the Mission Viejo move with an outpouring of creative energy. Much of it demonstrated her considerable wit. "To Kay and Herb – a Poetic Blurb" addressed the idiosyncrasies of life in a gated California community:

> It ain't a dog, it ain't a goat
> What you'll see will be a coyote!
> If you trip and slip, bless your soul,
> You've just found a gopher hole!
> And – if your house begins to quiver,
> Like Henry Ford's Model T Flivver,
> It is not Andreas Fault –
> It's just me – chopping liver!

"To Joan," another gem, surveyed the common ritual of weight reduction:

> Goals are achieved at sacrifice,
> Each pound that's lost extracts its price,
> Each once that's gained
> Is a pang that's pained.
> No French éclairs, no Scotch on ice?
>
> To achieve the term that's known as 'lean,'
> To avoid the labels known as 'queen,'
> To resist the bliss

Of a chocolate kiss,
And call a Danish illegal, obscene?

Oh, those goals I have to hurdle
To squeeze into a smaller girdle,
To fight, to conquer, and to force it,
My derriere into a corset
Is enough to make my thinned blood curdle.

Diet, diet, tears and laughter,
They call me 'nuts,' some think I'm dafter,
I'm up the hill
Like Jack and Jill,
I pray my pounds come tumbling after!

Dorothy's participation in Temple services and Bible classes led to her joining the local B'nai B'rith Women. Serving as the service organization's publicity director and publications editor, she turned to dramatic sketches to build chapter morale. In "Ladies of the Covenant," each prospect for the branch presidency bows out with a litany of retiree excuses:

I'm a library volunteer,
I'm in ceramics,
I'm in dramatics,
I'm having anguish,
With French and Spanish,
With dietetics,
And genetics,
My Mah Jong's on Monday,
My Pan is on Sunday,
Bowling – can't quit it,
Can't leave 'em short,
On the tennis court.

In the end, the women discover that the rabbi's wife is delighted to become their leader.

Beyond lighthearted skits, Dorothy incorporated her experience as a teacher and activist in devising informative presentations on Jewish history, women's rights, and social justice. "Women of Valor" honored Jewish female figures in history. Yet Dorothy was not content to focus on celebrated figures such as Anne Frank. Instead, her script told the story of unknowns including Rosalyn Yalow, a pioneering Yeshiva University radiation chemist; Anni Hazkelson, a near-forgotten child diarist lost in the Holocaust; and Clara Lemlich, a garment worker and labor activist who perished with 145 others in New York's Triangle Shirtwaist Company Fire of 1911.

Two additional sketches addressed the universal implications of Jewish ethics. "House of Miracles" dealt with an American Jewish women's charity group that supports an Israeli hospital that treats the wife of an accused Palestinian terrorist. In a similar vein, "The Jerusalem Connection" illustrated how children of all ethnic and religious backgrounds received care at the Israeli boys' home the B'nai B'rith chapter sponsored.

In spare time, Dorothy worked on personal projects. A short story, "The Grandfather's Clock," described a five-year-old boy's response to the losses of World War II and the Holocaust, but concludes by offering the regenerative power of hope. "Different" explored issues of autonomy with a woman who fears entrapment in a shadow of a marriage to an accountant – a "very respectable, respected moral relationship that could never hold up under the light of truth." In the end, she resolves the dilemma by welcoming a long sought-after pregnancy.

The affirmative tone of these pieces contrasted with darker themes. "Another Mistake" described an elderly retiree who reflects that her life is full of "little people with little lives filled with nothingness." Leading an existence based on early-bird dinners, gasohol pumps, stocks, and assessments of her condominium's sales value, she wonders if she is "playing at living."

"Busy, busy, the watchword of condo living," the narrator observes.

"Oh, brave new world for the old, where being alone constituted a crime."

"What do I want," she finally asks, "from a life that is ending?"

Another sketch, "Twilight Village," portrayed a widowed resident of a retirement community's sense of entrapment. Unable to sleep at 5 a.m., she reminds herself that she had to be careful because this was her home—her last home; these were her only friends. Ostracism or ridicule meant a slow death. One must play the game cheerfully: be pleasant, helpful, not too bright, not too good at anything.

Similar doubts marked "Leisure Land, California":

Gray-haired old ladies
In their black Mercedes
Drive through the hills
To pay telephone bills.
As dew sip their tulips,
They nip mint juleps,
And play-act until
Their hearts become still.

Soon a real-estate banner
Flaps over their manor,
And another gray lady
Rides her Mercedes,
And drives to her fate
On the Great Interstate.

Family Ties

In June 1982, less than a year after the move to Mission Viejo, Nat and Dorothy returned to Oregon to attend the Portland State Commencement to see Michael awarded his PhD. They now had two sons with doctorates. As David prepared for a second sabbatical, Nat and Dorothy helped him buy a used Datsun wagon that he drove to Casta del Sol in late August. As her son completed background reading and organized a cross-country research trip, Dorothy provided fresh daily lunches on the rear patio, making it appear as if family bonds had never severed.

When David resumed teaching a year later, Michael had retooled with a community college computer literacy course. He now signed on with a Bay Area friend's company to publish newsletters and organize conferences centered on marketing tools for independent physicians. The fact that the careers of both sons appeared to be thriving brought an immense sense of relief to their parents. By the spring of 1984, however, Dorothy's concerns about her brother were compromising her peace of mind.

In the years after Mickey Levine stepped down as national chair of the American Veterans Committee in 1961, he anguished over the organization's reluctance to criticize the military policies of the Kennedy and Johnson administrations. The complete break came in 1966 when AVC officially backed the Vietnam War. When Americans for Democratic Action signaled opposition to the conflict a year later, Mickey signed on as chair of its New York State Legislative Committee. This lasted until 1968, when ADA endorsed war hawk Vice-President Hubert Humphrey's race for the Democratic presidential nomination. Still, Mickey returned to ADA in 1971. Seeking to retool the organization with a social agenda attractive to Vietnam veterans, youth, and minorities, he agreed to become New York State Chair in 1973. When the old guard resisted these changes, however, Mickey resigned two years later and, in an interview, permitted a *New York Times* reporter to characterize ADA as "a paper tiger."

Mickey's disaffection from the two liberal affiliations framing his post-World War II political activism reflected a profound disillusionment with his own generation, most of whom he accused of selling out to powerful interests to enhance their careers. This sense of isolation intensified following his stroke in 1976, when he became increasingly critical of his employer, New York's Federation of Jewish Philanthropies. At first, Mickey antagonized fellow executives by supporting an employee labor walkout. Then he voiced furious objections to the charity's initial support of a state bill to fingerprint welfare recipients and its refusal to endorse legislation requiring police identification tags. Alleged financial ties between several Federation rabbis and substandard nursing homes presented another source of friction. After resigning in 1977, Mickey divided his time between part-time employment as a bookkeeper and volunteer work for the consumer boycott campaigns of the Amalgamated Clothing Workers and the United Farm Workers. He also participated in sit-ins against President Jimmy Carter's reinstatement of draft registration and Wall Street investments in the defense sector. In 1982, Mickey joined a historic gathering of 750,000 in Central Park to demand a bilateral Soviet and U.S. freeze on the production and deployment of nuclear weapons. Two days later, he faced arrest for his role in a "die-in" at the U.S. Mission to the United Nations. Objecting to the abrogation of his right to peaceful assembly, Mickey informed the night court that he would only disclose his name and World War II Army rank and serial number.

"As a prisoner of Ronald Reagan and Mayor [Ed] Koch and under the Articles of War," he announced, "I refuse all other information."

Mickey's new period of activism merely reinforced his political and social alienation.

"I just detest organized religion, the church, organized politics, society, organizations," he wrote David the day after Christmas in 1980.

Nothing could "inspire a man to hatred, fanaticism, terrorism, murder like God," he later commented. By now, Mickey had discarded all of his picture albums, plaques, newspaper stories, and mementos, including an early American Veterans Committee group photo in which he appeared with one-time member Ronald Reagan, now the Republican president of the United States. Even David could not escape his wrath.

"Professors shouldn't be allowed to write, they do enough damage in the classroom," he complained when his nephew began to pursue the history of populist conservatives.

Americans, Mickey advised, were "inherent racists, approve of a draft ..., despise the aged and the poor, idealize teenage imbecility ..., and worship money."

By 1984, Mickey's fortunes had taken a turn for the worse. First, he failed to prevail in a malpractice suit against the hospital that had operated on his gallbladder. The resulting stroke, he contended to no avail, had been the product of an improperly administered anesthetic. Not long after, he lost his bookkeeping job. To add to his difficulties, Mickey was experiencing severe angina.With his defenses down, he gave into his sister's pleading and agreed to move to California to be close to the only family he had.

That summer, Nat and Dorothy found a ground-floor apartment for the inveterate New Yorker in Leisure World and helped him set up housekeeping. Yet it did not take long for him to issue venomous denunciations of his Orange County counterparts as selfish and useless Ronald Reaganites, a description that included the friends and neighbors of his sister and brother-in-law. Mickey even claimed that the foggy, cold, and damp California weather and continual boredom drove him to consuming sweets and smoking reams of cigars, dangerous indulgences given his diabetic and heart problems. He changed his mind from hour to hour and made completely irrational statements, driving Dorothy to tears, Nat reported to David. It was no surprise, therefore, that by the spring of 1985, Mickey had resolved to leave California to go to Florida.

He would "die with the old Jews," he announced.

Warriors

Once Mickey arrived in North Miami Beach, where he found a cheerful garden apartment along a canal, he claimed to be a new person. Yet his California sojourn had left a toll. Beyond immense frustration with her brother, Dorothy had to contend with Nat's increasing dependence upon a walker and the physical pains and discomforts associated with his various maladies. Meanwhile, she valiantly prepared meals and entertained a succession of house guests despite periodic cramps and bouts of diarrhea. Nat chose to believe that his wife remained her usual cheerful self throughout the ordeal. Yet a series of diagnostic tests during the winter of 1985 revealed a malignant intestinal tumor.

In April, a surgeon successfully removed twelve inches of tubing from Dorothy's colon. In gratitude, Nathan sent a $1,000 donation to the Temple. Yet the cancer had penetrated the abdominal walls and entered the lymph nodes. Nat now geared himself up for the fight of his life. Refusing to succumb to any negativity, he prevailed on cousin Mo Golub to elicit a referral from his son Sidney, a leading cancer researcher at the University of California at Los Angeles. Dorothy now became an outpatient at UCLA's John Wayne Clinic.

The center's Hollywood benefactor, Michael pointed out, offered the perfect exemplar of the warrior mentality required to confront a completely ruthless disease.

8

SUNLIGHT AND SHADOWS

By June 1985, Dorothy had inaugurated a low-fat diet, pursued a routine of rigorous daily walking, and following Michael's New Age counsel, absorbed the treatises of holistic cancer surgeon, Dr. Bernie Segal. When David visited at the close of the school year, Dorothy insisted that he keep up his academic work and prepared meals as if nothing had changed. Nevertheless, doctors informed her in August that the cancer had spread to the liver. Back at UCLA, she underwent a second operation to remove the tumor and hoped for the best.

Not Yet

Dorothy's illness seemed to inspire her most evocative poetry. Like Nat, she felt awed by the beauty and strength of the California landscape. In "Saddleback Mountain," she mixed an appreciation of Nature's wonders with a reflective dose of humility:

> The layers of hills recede
> In the fog,
> They have a need
> To talk with God
> In shrouded privacy.
>
> I am made to feel a stranger
> And wonder what they say
> To each other, so secret,
> As the sun hovers near.
>
> They shut me out, an alien
> Yet I hear their whispers
> From the summit
> And begin to fear their plan for Man.
>
> A quake to shake the earth?
> A flood of rain?
> A slide of mud?
> A mountain writhing in volcanic fire?
> But when they appear again
> With bonnet-caps of snow,
> I can only marvel
> At their calm and majesty
> Leaning at peace against the sky.

Another poem, "The Golden Weed," acknowledged the preciousness of all life forms:

> Dandelions, you know
> Are merely weeds.
> As they grow
> All buttery yellow
> They must be filling
> Someone's needs.

Why do you spray
These golden flowers,
Must they die
Because they are weeds?
Let them grow and multiply
Let them welcome the morning ray
Must we all be gorgeous orchids?

Similar sentiment characterized "I Cannot Bear to Crush a Rose":

Even when a petal falls,
I cannot bear to crush a rose.
I cannot bear a crumpled rose,
Even when the pinkness palls.

Even with the fragrance gone,
And brown decay begins to show,
I know, I must discard them finally,
And give new buds a chance to grow,
I know . . . I know . . .
But I cannot come to crush a rose.

Facing a second surgery, Dorothy collected her thoughts in "Not Yet":

There are too many things to say today,
So many lines to write tonight.
The world with all its prettiness,
Life, despite its pettiness,
            is precious.

Let me go with dignity
I will not grieve
When I leave my three beloved,
Nathan, Michael, and Avram David —
No – No – Not Yet!
I shall fight and kick and scream
And mutter syllables obscene
And rail against my fate
That eager Death could not wait!

I shall go with dignity,
For what must be – will be!

Softly, pull the plug please,
My mind is now at ease.
Say Kaddish – and when it is said,
Throw three roses at my head.

Peace Talk

As chemotherapy treatments continued during the summer of 1986, Dorothy learned that Mickey had experienced a second, massive stroke. Unable to travel, she dispatched David to Hollywood Memorial Hospital in Florida, where her father had died thirteen years earlier. David found Mickey barely responsive except for periodic rants at the doctors and nurses for putting him through hell. Finally, David responded that no one could give another person a reason for living but he was there if his uncle needed help. That proved to be the turning point. The patient soon mastered the use and cleaning of his new electric razor, acclimated to his temporary walker, and learned to turn on the shower and dress by himself.

Once returning home, Mickey even gained new respect for his sister when in a phone call he wondered if political reactionaries were truly vicious or simply morons.

"They're vicious morons!" Dorothy replied.

When David sent on an extended account of his participation in a tour of socialist Nicaragua the following spring that warned against U.S. meddling, Mickey distributed the piece to the entire South Florida congressional delegation.

"Congratulations! You are your grandmother's boy after all," he wrote.

"Great work—I'm proud of you. Take back all the insults."

The Middle East remained the family's most divisive issue. Both Dorothy and Nat agreed the Israelis ultimately would have to make peace with the Arabs. Dorothy even confessed she lost sleep for several nights in September 1982 when Israel's Christian militia allies in Lebanon carried out a massacre of hundreds of women and children at a Palestinian refugee camp. Yet as five-time visitors to Israel well versed in the Palestine Liberation Organization's record of terrorist crimes, the couple strenuously defended Tel Aviv's refusal to negotiate with PLO leader Yasir Arafat, whom they deeply mistrusted. Back in 1976, Mickey had relayed a Portland United Jewish Appeal official's comment that David had a reputation as a "radical pro-Arab." Mindful of Nat's chronic hypertension, Dorothy discouraged family discussions of the matter.

Despite their differences, Nat and Dorothy had more influence on their sons than seemed apparent. A pivotal transition for David came in the fall of 1985 when an armed PLO team took over an Italian cruise ship and tossed an elderly, wheelchair-bound Jewish man overboard. Given his father's increasing reliance on a walker, David had difficulty coming to terms with the atrocity. When a Palestinian student subsequently published a generic condemnation of Zionism in the Portland State newspaper, David countered with a sharply worded rebuttal. Gratuitous violence and sterile rhetoric were not substitutes for substantive dialogue over the Middle East conflict, he wrote. The university should hold an open debate on the issue, he insisted.

While prodding Palestinian activists and the student government to follow up on the proposal, David joined the local chapter of New Jewish Agenda, an organization of young professionals who billed themselves as the progressive voice in the Jewish community and the Jewish voice in the progressive movement. For David, the affiliation offered useful support for his peace efforts but also honored Nat's plea that his sons never forget their heritage.

The promised debate, held before an audience of 450 people, including a large number of international students, took place in early June 1986. Anxious to get beyond an "us versus them" mindset, David and the president of the Jewish Student Union introduced a variation on the "two-state" solution. The proposal called for acknowledgment of Israel's unequivocal rights of sovereignty and security in exchange for the recognition of a Palestinian state in the Occupied Territories with issues like Jerusalem and refugees to be decided in subsequent negotiations. David's goal was to publicize a midway position between the Palestinian movement and his parents' loyalties. The strategy had a modest effect. While he garnered enhanced respect among several Palestinian students at the university, his efforts helped prompt an invitation from Nat and Dorothy to deliver two public talks on Jewish issues in Mission Viejo.

David used the first occasion, an open meeting of the men's B'nai B'rith lodge in June 1987, to present a description of the historic relationship between Jews and reform in the United States. Speaking on "American Jews and the Progressive World Challenge" at the Temple a few days later, he pleaded for the extension of Jewish traditions of compassion toward the powerless. In the Middle East, David argued, Jews did not belong in the camp of those who wielded power without concern for its consequences. The challenge of revolutionary change in the world required the Jewish people to do more than protect narrow interests, he concluded.

Although David had presented the case for a two-state solution, his experience in dealing with his parents enabled him to avoid talking down to a Jewish audience, most of whom appeared appreciative of a respectful effort to promote dialogue. This seemed sufficient for Nat and Dorothy, who expressed pride in their son's performance. When David returned the next month, he attended a joint installation ceremony of his parents' respective B'nai B'rith lodges.

In September 1987, as Dorothy's illness appeared in remission, she and Nat visited Portland, where David was performing as a backstage piano player for a production of *Ma Rainey's Black Bottom*, a prize-winning drama about a 1920s African American blues band. Years earlier, David had served as keyboardist for the company's summer vaudeville and burlesque shows, an ironic throwback to his parents' roots. To help finance his second divorce, moreover, he had taken a gig at Bogart's Joint, a 1940s nostalgia tavern. Having spent much of her youth in a seedy cabaret, Dorothy had misgivings about a college professor playing for tips at a beer joint. Yet *Ma Rainey* turned out to be an enormous success. Never an easy critic, the former Nat Harris marveled at the troupe's spirit and professionalism.

Figarow

While in Portland, Nat and Dorothy visited the carriage house that David rented behind a Victorian Gothic mansion. Nat assured David that if he ever wanted to "settle down," he and Dorothy would help finance a home. Weeks later, the owners revealed they had sold the property to a couple who intended to build a garage to the rear of the lot. David now asked a realtor friend to keep an eye out for a "rustic" place. Not long after, she produced a three-bedroom, log-sided house on a wooded Northeast Portland double lot with a living room wood stove set in a river rock backing, intricate cabinet work, and tongue-and-groove cedar paneling. Although Nat appreciated the home's charm, he raised concerns about the lack of a second bathroom, the transitional nature of the neighborhood, and insufficient light from the dense foliage. Interested, however, in a potential refuge for Michael, he and Dorothy agreed to fund half the sales price.

In January 1988, David moved into the house with Gloria, a returning History student whose Polish Catholic parents had operated a Connecticut dairy farm. Days later, he drove to California. Nat had checked in at UCLA for surgery to repair lower back degeneration and painful compression on the spinal nerves—a result of the severe lumbar stenosis now limiting his mobility. Despite lingering discomfort, however, the patient resumed a hectic pace of activity within weeks. Having failed to find a venue for "My *Feh* Lady," Nat proceeded to devote his time to producing a "non-ethnic" version of the cross-dressing "mock marriage" he had fashioned in the Catskills nearly thirty-five years ago.

Nat Horowitz was a hard taskmaster, although Dorothy remained baffled that the soft-hearted and sentimental man she knew could intimidate anyone. By July, at any rate, he had cajoled his amateur cast into shape. Staged as a Temple fundraiser, "The Marriage of Don Geeva Figarow" reworked its creator's penchant for raucous parody. This time, a generic "reverend" presided over the nuptials with the retirees of Casta del Sol serving as the congregation.

The ceremony opened by poking fun at the one-upmanship of the elderly ushers and bridesmaids, who march down the aisle to a parody of the "The Battle Hymn of the Republic":

> This one's got a grandson who's a whiz at Harvard Law,
> This one's got a piker for a lousy son-in-law,
> And that one's got a genius like you never saw before.
> This one has a bankroll that is bigger than Fort Knox,
> That one he indulges in pizza, tacos, lox
> This one is a lecher who goes pinching Goldilox ...

Another number, a recycled version of *Oklahoma*'s "The Farmer and the Cowman," which Nat formerly had used to describe the homeowners of Long Island's North and South Shore, now took on the residents of Casta del Sol's two subdivisions:

The Carmels and Fiestas must be friends,
The Carmels and Fiestas must be friends,
No matter from what state you hail,
California's now your jail,
So all together we must be friends.

"Figarow" lacked the lyrical precision and emotional nuance of "My *Feh* Lady." Even so, following a thunderous curtain call, admirers flocked to congratulate Nat and praise the grace and poise with which a radiant Dorothy had carried off her role as narrator. Yet few of those who marveled at the star performer's appearance realized that she was due to resume chemotherapy at UCLA the following morning. Certainly, it seemed something of a stretch to honor the Broadway tradition that the show must go on. Yet laughter, as the holistic physicians liked to say, offered one of the most lucrative paths to healing.

Here!

Two months after the show, Nat and Dorothy returned to Portland. By September 1988, David was in the last stages of a campaign against a university president who sought to build the institution's reputation around intercollegiate football and ties to the business community. With Gloria's assistance, he had followed his father's footsteps by fashioning a scathing parody to "Chattanooga Choo-Choo," one of the president's favorites. Ever protective of her son, Dorothy worried that the professor's role in the struggle might jeopardize his academic status. Having won a full professorship a year earlier and been careful to elicit the support of colleagues, however, David was not in jeopardy. Weeks later, the State Board of Higher Education orchestrated the official's resignation.

Sometime before Nat and Dorothy arrived in Portland, David sent several of their recent writings to Mike McCusker, publisher of Astoria, Oregon's alternative *North Coast Times Eagle*. In September, McCusker ran Nat's "Dedication of the Ark" and Dorothy's "The Survivor" — a one-act play detailing a conversation between a cancer patient, her brain, and her surgeon.

After the doctor diagnoses the presence of a malignancy, the body's T. Cells report the growth of a tumor in the brain's frontal lobe. The brain then sends out the alarm for white corpuscles to eliminate its adversaries. One of the "White Corps," Colonel Killer, explains that the mutated cells "just went bad ... their DNA's confused." Yet Killer is reluctant to eradicate the "good" cells in the process of eliminating the bad ones.

This precipitates an appeal from the patient. "Colonel, sir," she pleads,

> haven't I supplied you with nutrients, oxygen, all these years? 98.6 degrees in all kinds of weather? We've seen the Louvre, the Parthenon, the Pyramids, Laguna Beach. I've never abused you with nicotine, alcohol, drugs.Don't be an ingrate! Give me a break! Nuke 'em!

In support of the patient's plea, another member of the White Corps points out that the mutants are taking food from the good, hardworking cells.

"They reproduce like bunnies," he explains. "They have no sense of morality, no boundaries. They keep spreading.... And Killer, remember, they are in the strategic part of the body ... in the Brain!"

The patient then pleads with the battalion that the attack is "for our body, our team, our very existence... for science!"

Following successful treatment, an Epilogue finds the survivor reclining on her southern California patio in a sun hat and beach robe, pad and pencil in hand.

Why not enjoy life, the brain inquires? She responds that there could be another crisis. Dealing with cancer, she explains, is "living with a time bomb."

The survivor then recites a poem entitled "Reprieve," that Dorothy had composed after a third hospitalization:

> My senses are keener –
> The soft silk of a pink petal –
> The perfume makes me dizzy –
> The ecstasy of a piano concerto –
> Smooth white wine –
> The crunch of a walnut.
>
> The walk up a hill –
> And survey the valley –

And of all wonders,
To hold your hand,
To laugh, to smile together,
And say, "I am here!
Oh, I am here!"

Believing

Moved by "Survivor," McCusker published Dorothy's "A Baseball Fan Fights Cancer" in October 1988. The piece traced the diamond's mythic role in the family's history. During her Bronx childhood of the 1920s, when as a tomboy she was the lone girl on the all-boys' baseball team, she recalled, the Levines rooted for the "proletarian" Yankees in contrast to the "upper-crust" New York Giants. When Dorothy met fervid Giant fan Nat, however, she vowed she would "not let this guy get away" and switched allegiance.

"The result of our marriage contract," she explained, "was the unwritten law, 'Thou Shall Be A Giants Fan Unto the Second Generation'."

Dorothy's favorite Yankee had been Babe Ruth. She remembered seeing the emaciated former slugger take a suitcase out of a car on a Manhattan street years after he had retired and been stricken with cancer. A radio broadcast would announce Ruth's demise on David's seventh birthday. By 1951, the year of Bobby Thomson's celebrated home run, however, the Horowitz household was fixated on the fate of the Giants.

By the time Dorothy wrote her feature, Thomson's feat was an integral part of family lore. The radio call of the pennant-winning blast had served as the inspiration for the lead character's attempt to defy insignificance in *Tin Waltz*. "Heroicide Americanus," a retrospective Michael published in a Portland literary magazine three years after the eventful spring of 1968, pictured Bobby Thomson rounding the bases in triumph only to have Dodger pitcher Ralph Branca turn into an angry Arab who shoots "Bobby" before he can get to home plate. Then, in December 1986, *The Forward* ran Nat's "G-d and the World Series, which pictured David's mother dispatching him to Hebrew School in deference to her husband's expectations.

Dorothy's version let Nat have his say but recycled David's recollection that she simply could not bear to witness her son's despair as the Dodgers surged ahead in the top of the ninth. She then recalled how the Giants

155

lost the World Series to the rival Yankees in 1951 but returned to the Fall Classic three years later to sweep Cleveland in four games.

In 1958, however, the fabled squad from Coogan's Bluff deserted New York for San Francisco, leaving a legacy of betrayal that would only begin to heal when the New York Mets opened shop in the early Sixties.

The irony of it all, Dorothy points out, was now that she lived in California, the Los Angeles Dodgers had become her team. Yet these days, baseball had a new role.

"The crux of my story is that I now have cancer," she wrote – "the chemotherapy, the side-effects, the surgery, the diagnostic tests, the whole miserable deal."

Baseball was her therapy and salvation, Dorothy confides, particularly when she could not tolerate the brutality and inhumanity depicted in full color television newscasts.

The news was "too stressful," she insisted, "and stress interferes with the body's natural immunity system, my prime hope for a cure."

Instead of taking a sleeping pill, Dorothy recounts, she listens to the literate and cheerful voice of Dodgers radio announcer Vince Scully.

"Remember, when you watch a game," she explains,

> you are not the one who is out stealing. You are not striking out with two on...someone else is making the mistake for a change. And a goat can become a hero in the next inning. When the Mets' McReynolds hits a grand slammer in the bottom of the ninth to win a game – well, miracles do happen. That makes me think, one miracle for you, McReynolds, the next one for me. When Doc Gooden strikes out the side, what if I clap my hands and yell "Yah!" It is therapeutic. It gets my good cells, the T-cells, moving to attack the damned cancer cells ... baseball is my first love. Baseball is going to help me get well. I know it. I watch a game and remember when I was healthy. I remember to believe in miracles. Weren't the Giants thirteen and a half games behind in August once?

The recollection ends with the memory of David hitting a home run that reached the huckleberry bushes at the edge of the Fink's Bungalows softball field the same day a herd of dairy cows improbably invaded third base.

"You gotta believe!" concludes Dorothy, a reference to the rallying cry of the New York Mets World Series Champions of 1973.

Roots

As David and Gloria undertook preparations for a cross-country auto trip in June 1989, the *North Coast Times Eagle* published Nat's poem, "Keep Off the Grass." The verse sounded the theme that beauty in the limitless wastes was there for admiration, not touching. If humans did not respect the natural wonders of the mountains, seas, deserts, jungles, and the air, it warned, they would face dire circumstances:

> Your brainy boys who stand so proud
> With squeaking chalk stubs in their hands,
> Will calculize, computerize,
> And squint their eyes,
> And pinch their brows,
> And with brilliant quotients find, your final, fatal doom.

Publication of the poem coincided with an anti-pollution battle over an area bordering the Columbia Slough, a half-mile away from David's Portland house. A Korean firm had announced plans to access copper components by burning off electrical transformer residues at an incinerator at the site. In response, the neighborhood association elicited testimony that the PCB compounds and dioxin by-products of such a process could be potentially carcinogenic.

Given Dorothy's ongoing battles, David reacted forcefully.

"We will not allow ourselves to become guinea pigs at the risk of our health and safety," he insisted in a statement read at a subsequent hearing. No amount of corporate puffery, he warned, could protect the safety of outside financial interests preparing to poison the community.

Whether in reaction to citizen outcries or a result of mere bureaucratic shuffling, the Oregon Department of Environmental Quality soon turned the matter over to the Portland Planning Bureau, which ultimately ruled that the site's proximity to the Columbia Slough disqualified it from a land-use permit.

Days later, David, Gloria, and Gloria's thirteen-year-old son David set out in the Datsun for Connecticut, where Gloria's mother lived in a small home on the farm grounds. On route, the travelers stopped at several major league baseball parks. Yet family history was the main agenda.

On July 4th, the trio found themselves on the main street of Honesdale, Pennsylvania at the corner where the Levines ran their first Chinese restaurant. Crossing the Delaware River, they made their way to Lake Huntington, where they speculated where Nat Levine's Broadway Casino might have stood and tried to find the lakeside spot where Nady and Dorothy first met. Ten miles away in White Lake, they proceeded to the site of Fink's Bungalows, now a barbed wire-enclosed Hasidic Jewish compound. Gloria snapped a photo of David tossing a rubber ball on the abandoned softball diamond. The "field of dreams" trip extended to a visit to the West Bronx, where only rubble remained where 1495 Popham Avenue once stood and most of the neighborhood appeared in ruins. In Riverdale, David put in a claim to Aunt Teddy for future custody of a framed photo of his great-grandfather and namesake, Abraham David Golub.

Bread and Butter Lines

When David and Gloria returned to Mission Viejo in late summer of 1989, a brand new Chrysler sedan sat in the garage. The purchase was partly an act of faith—a reflection of Nat and Dorothy's anticipation of an extended future together. They also had embarked on a new project — "Pieces of Nate" — a typescript anthology of 110 of Nat's poems "culled from the years." Published as a Jewish New Year's gift for friends and family under the rubric of Barnebec Press, a tribute to Barnett and Becky, the collection featured a cover photograph of the couple with their heads lovingly tilted against each other.

Just as "Pieces of Nate" made its way to the copy center, Michael sent on his first work of fiction. After serving as a journalist for a health industry weekly and putting in a stint with a Bay Area firm marketing computer systems for academic libraries, Michael had returned to Portland to pursue creative writing. Rebuffed by New York presses, he incorporated *Times Eagle Books* with Mike McCusker as its publisher and assumed the pseudonym, V. O. Blum. *Equator: The Story and the Letters* (1989), billed as an "Erotic New Age Novel," followed a Greek American agricultural specialist to West Africa, where he enters an intricate web of relationships with a Norwegian male adventurer and an older Dutch woman who combines a passion for advanced mathematics and metaphysics with a taste for bodily pleasures.

Michael had warned his parents of the book's quirky sexuality.

"I was a guidance counselor," Dorothy wrote back. "There's nothing that shocks me."

Despite her protests, the tale's New Age characters and formulations were difficult for an older generation to relate to, a problem Mickey experienced as well. Meanwhile, Dorothy was in a rough patch of waters. In March, the *North Coast Times Eagle* had published her "Welcome: Do Not Enter," a light-hearted account of her years in guidance. Yet Dorothy subsequently experienced two psychological setbacks. Weeks after the fact, she learned that Laura, her best friend in high school, had died without anyone informing her. Then her irreverent B'nai B'rith cohort Bea suffered a fatal stroke while undergoing a routine sinus operation. Dorothy intended to recite "Leisure Land, California," a verse whose capriciousness had appealed to Bea's wry humor, at the memorial, only to have a lodge sister ask her to omit the selection as inappropriate.

By summer, a home aide was preparing meals and cleaning while Dorothy dealt with anemia, high blood pressure, heart problems, diminished lung capacity, and other consequences of both the cancer and chemotherapy. It is not surprising that this period generated some of her most poignant poetry. For example, a tinge of regret colored the lines of "What Happened?"

> What happened to April?
> Some spots of sunshine I recall,
> Some rain at times began to fall.
> I think that's all.
> What happened to my life?
> Two sons, a friend or two –
> And you, as I recall.
> That is all.

"Bread-and-Butter Lines" offered succinct final thoughts:

> Thank you, world, for having me,
> Thanks for the fancy cake and tea.
> It was a feast –
> To say the least –
> A great party!
> But – then –
> I know I won't be invited again!

The Pact

While David and Gloria visited, Dorothy jumped at the chance to join them for a California Angels baseball game when a neighbor produced free tickets. Delighted to be among the living, she bravely insisted on enjoying each moment of the outing even when the opponents scored seven runs in the top of the first inning in a lopsided rout. By the time David and Gloria returned in December, however, repeated chemotherapy had taken its toll. The most obvious consequence was a loss of appetite, forcing her, at Nat's desperate urging, to consume a flavored nutritional drink she detested. As Dorothy shuttled between doctors and therapy in a weakened state, she appeared to be on an irreversible slide. Weeks later, she insisted on paying off the remaining balance on David's Portland mortgage.

In June 1990, a month after the *North Coast Times Eagle* published Dorothy's "Twilight Village," she prompted David to see an attorney to draw up papers empowering him as co-proprietor of a family trust. As her husband and son ran errands to assemble the financial portfolio or broke up the day with rides in the eastern hills, Dorothy confided in Gloria.

Her chief concern was Nat, who seemed unable to deal with the seriousness of her illness and panicked at any hint of abandonment. His defensiveness even induced suppressed giggles when nearly every movie video rental threatened to violate his instructions that no feature include a reference to death or dying. Learning that Gloria planned to attend her niece's wedding in Connecticut, Dorothy presented her with the airfare. One afternoon when Nat sought temporary relief from arthritic pain with a visit to the Jacuzzi and swimming pool, Dorothy asked David if he and Gloria planned to marry. When he nodded hesitantly, she returned the gesture.

Not long after David and Gloria returned to Oregon, Nat called to report that Dorothy had suffered a cardiac episode during an MRI exam and required hospitalization. Once David flew to California, his mother's condition stabilized but he agreed to return for an extended August stay during the home aid's vacation. By then, Dorothy was considerably weaker, partly a result of the supply of morphine painkillers her doctor had placed at her disposal. Instead of struggling into the den to watch baseball on television, she seemed content to listen to the broadcasts on the bedside radio. One morning she told David of a dream in which her deceased father waved as if welcoming her. On another occasion, she asked her older son to look out after Mickey.

Dorothy and David had an unstated pact calling for her to endure the outcome of events at home. One afternoon, the visiting nurse took David aside to warn that not much time remained and that he needed to make sure final arrangements were in order. Every day, in fact, appeared to bring a new crisis. A point of no return seemed to come on the morning Nat called David to the master bathroom where Dorothy had fallen. As he lifted his mother from the floor, her nightgown opened up. Believing she had embarrassed him, she apologized.

That evening, Dorothy asked the visiting nurse for a bath, only to learn that the aide was behind schedule with other appointments. Five minutes later, the doorbell rang. The caregiver had reconsidered. Dorothy told her she was a guardian angel.

Sometime after midnight, David awoke to Nat's insistent call from the other end of the house. When he came into the fully lit bedroom, Dorothy's head rested upright against the bed pillows. Her eyes closed, she exhaled heavily with a mechanical monotony. Nat tried to arouse her but got no response. Not long after, Dorothy took a last rattled breath. A dark mass of blood oozed out of the corner of her mouth. Instinctively, David cleansed it with a tissue.

For fifty-five years, Dorothy had served as Nathan's inspiration and protector. She had awakened him to the ways of the world, served as a beacon of social justice, sparked his creative efforts, been supportive of his work life, shared his reverses and disappointments, and provided an unqualified outpouring of love that few ever warrant.

Dorothy had endured her five and a half years of illness with steadfast courage.

Now the couple's storied romance finally was over.

She was six months past her seventy-third birthday. He was nearly eighty-two.

Screaming in rage, Nathan made a final attempt to vent his will on a cruel and uncaring universe. Then his body went limp and he fell helplessly back on the twin bed.

9

FATE

By pre-arrangement, the Newport Beach funeral home arranged for a group of Hasidic followers to conduct a ritualistic cleansing of Dorothy's body before burial. Hours after the brilliant southern California sun rose on Friday, August 24th, Nat and David made the silent drive to the mortuary to pick out a casket. Following Jewish tradition, which requires internment in a wooden box so the remains are free to return to earth, they chose a simple but dignified dark walnut container. The service took place on Sunday before a packed sanctuary. It included the rabbi's reading of a tribute from Teddy Mass heralding her sister-in-law as a "class lady." A message from Mickey Levine celebrated Dorothy's service as a teacher, union member, peace activist, and human rights champion. The ceremony concluded with an audiotape of Frank Sinatra's "Young at Heart," a Fifties classic Michael remembered as one of his mother's favorites.

Hegira

Respecting the request in the closing line of "Not Yet," David, Gloria, and Michael each tossed a yellow rose into the grave. Following the funeral, the family sat *shivah*—the seven day period of mourning in which friends and family pay respects, provide home cooked delicacies, and join in *Kaddish* prayers for the departed. During his Roslyn Heights days, Nat had completed two short stories about surviving widowers. Yet as he approached his eighty-second birthday, nothing could penetrate his despair over losing his loving partner of more than a half-century.

By what standard of justice, he agonized, could he have survived his beloved Dorothy, nearly nine years his junior, when by all rights he should have been the first to go?

David took his father on long afternoon rides in the Chrysler. Yet Nat's physical maladies only reinforced his depression. By this time, he had plastic implants on both hips, had undergone a quadruple bypass after a cardiac arrest, and despite spinal surgery, continued suffering from rheumatoid arthritis. Exclusively reliant on a walker, he experienced vascular abnormalities that left him with aching legs, burning knees, and swollen ankles. Meanwhile, the steroids and drugs designed to alleviate these symptoms, including the pills he once referred to as "narcotic lollipops," produced facial lesions, burning skin, nausea, and other maladies.

Once David returned to Portland to resume teaching, a visiting nurse called daily at the Mission Viejo house while a home aid provided weekday meals and light housekeeping. Both sons made weekend visits as often as possible. Since the young Mexican-American aide spoke little English, however, and Nat barely heard her when she peered out of a magazine to say something, his isolation and loneliness only intensified. Facing an untenable situation, David entered negotiations with the Robison Jewish Home (now Cedar Sinai Park), a highly reputable kosher residential facility for the elderly in Portland's Raleigh Hills.

With Nathan's investment, pension, and social security income as a resource, David settled on a cheerful private corner suite with windows looking out in two directions. The unit would be roomy enough to hold a sampling of Nat's furniture and paintings as well his stereo, record collection, photographs, and entire personal archive. Intent on preserving his father's pride and sense of autonomy, David declined to apply for Medicaid nursing home coverage—an arrangement requiring the relinquishment of the resident's financial assets. After the family trust paid for a handicap shower, however, he petitioned Medicare to absorb the $3,000 cost of a power wheelchair to ensure his father's access to the upper floor dining room.

In mid-October, a crowd of thirty people gathered on the front patio of the Portland house for a reading of Dorothy's writings. David opened the proceedings by describing the young Dorothy Levine as an idealist who first took to pen in the 1930s to express her inner thoughts and passion for social justice. Then David and Michael read a number of selections from *Bread and Butter Lines*, a freshly assembled typescript publication of Dorothy's work that featured a facsimile of her 1939 World's Fair photo-identity card on the cover. Friends who received a copy of the collection could honor the author with a donation to the B'nai B'rith Home for Israeli and Palestinian boys. Appropriately, the reading concluded with a Jewish deli sampling of fish spread, bagels, cream cheese, and apple juice.

Days later, David and Gloria set out in a twenty-four-foot rental truck with an attached car trailer on the 1050-mile trek to Mission Viejo. The morning after arriving, David placed Nat on a plane to Portland and a temporary stay at the house with Michael. Meanwhile, Gloria and a team of B'nai B'rith brothers began packing the contents of the five-room condominium. David and Gloria then drove the truck with the Chrysler in tow back to Portland, where most of the furniture made its way to storage. When they escorted Nat and some of his possessions to Robison days later, the car assumed a position in the parking lot visible from the dining room, ready for the "jailbreaks" David promised to arrange three or four afternoons a week.

The New and the Old

Michael now flew in for twice-monthly visits from the Bay Area, where he had taken a position as executive editor of a media placement newsletter for public relations practitioners. For his part, David visited his father on free Tuesday and Thursday afternoons, plus once or twice on weekends. Excursions in the Chrysler frequently included lunch at a favorite Jewish deli, where Nat, now addressed at the Home as Nathan, broke his low-fat, no salt diet for pickled herring and sour cream or pastrami sandwiches on rye. On other occasions, the two sampled the *falafel, hummus,* grape leaf dishes, pita bread, and Turkish coffee at a downtown Lebanese eatery that rekindled Nat's memories of Jerusalem's Arab street vendors. David even took his father to some city league softball games involving his struggling "Wet Sox" team.

As long as he was out of the Home, Nathan was content to read in the car during errands to the central library, to stationery suppliers for typewriter ribbons, to the dry cleaners for items needing special care, or to the organic food market for almonds for his morning cereal. Meanwhile, David sought to keep his father engaged by reporting all that occurred in his life, including his scholarly aspirations in American cultural history. Nathan even came around to accepting his older son's insistence on remaining in the classroom and not seeking a department chair's responsibilities and bureaucratic headaches.

In March, David brought his father to Reed College for a conference on East European Jewry organized by Portland Rabbi Joshua Stampfer. David's audiovisual presentation, "Radun: The Life of Polish Jewish Village between the Wars," told the story of Becky's glass-lantern slides. Shortly before Dorothy's death, Nathan had turned over the photographic prints. After a Klezmer musician friend translated the attached Yiddish inscriptions, David had the set converted to plastic slides. At Nathan's suggestion, he contacted the Texas branch of the Golub family, who possessed a second series of pictures from Becky's sister Eva. The family's research revealed that experts evaluated the photographs as the most extensive documentation of a single Jewish village in interwar Poland, if not all Europe. Combining both collections, David donated a set of prints to New York's Yivo Museum of East European Jewish culture.

Newspaper clippings from Texas described Radun's cruel fate. In the early twentieth century, Rabbi Chofetz Hayim had discouraged emigration from the homeland, fearing a loss of traditional Jewish values in the materially oriented West. Yet in the final year before he died in 1933 at age ninety-four, the rabbi spoke of "a great menace coming upon the Jewish world within the next few years" that would "lead to the deaths of many Jews." Although the prophecy held out the ultimate survival of the Jewish people, it induced many followers to emigrate.

For those who remained, the consequences were severe. In April 1942, an elite SS regiment of Nazi troops entered Radun. A few survivors testified that Stormtroopers placed the entire Jewish population in a ghetto—a single row of houses surrounded by barbed wire. The punishment of death awaited any infraction of Occupation rules, including possession of meat or butter. In May, the troops gathered groups of villagers before a mass grave on the edge of town.

Using pistols, rifles, and machine guns, the regiment spent three days and nights systematically executing 1,175 men, women, and children.

As bulldozers and fires destroyed the homes, farms, businesses, and religious institutions captured in the Radun photographs, a survivor heard a German officer proclaim, "Let their names and their memories be erased from the face of the Earth."

Two years after the *aktion*—the Nazi term for mobile killing operations—soldiers from the Soviet Union retook the village, destroying its meager remains.

Once Too Often

During mid-winter of 1991, Nathan took a bad fall on the way to the bathroom. The Home now transferred him to the nursing wing for additional supervision. Petrified at the prospect, he convinced the staff to provide a private room by the main foyer, separating him at a reasonable distance from the general population. Nevertheless, increasing dependence on others made it very difficult to cut ties with the past. This became obvious when the last connection with Nathan's former life—the Mission Viejo condominium—came up for sale.

Despite his father's repeated objections, David followed the California realtor's advice and had the entire residence repainted and freshly carpeted. Then he ignored Nathan's outcry and listed the house at a mere $45,000 above its purchase price ten years earlier. Once an offer materialized, David quickly accepted despite Nathan's insistence that the bid was too low. The former Mission Viejo resident never retreated from this position even when a savings-and-loan crisis soon devastated the California real estate market and property values plummeted.

Not long after the house closed in the spring, Nathan and David flew to Newport Beach to join Michael for the unveiling of Dorothy's tombstone as prescribed by Jewish custom. A small group, including Sid Golub and friends from the Temple and Casta del Sol, gathered as the rabbi conducted the brief ritual. Beneath Dorothy's name and the years spanning her life, the inscription on the simple bronze plaque read "MOTHER WIFE TEACHER."

Later that year, David published a retrospective in a newsletter entitled *Back to the Bronx*. Recalling the residents of 1495 Popham Avenue, neighborhood culture, and even Bobby Thomson's home run, the piece concluded with the confession that all David's dreams of home took place in the old neighborhood. Nostalgia may have had something to do with the celebration of his fiftieth birthday that August. Yet the date happened to coincide with the first *Yahrzeit*—the Hebrew calendar anniversary of Dorothy's death and Nathan was in little mood to socialize when Michael wheeled him into the outdoor celebration at the Portland house.

Just as Nathan's spirits seemed beyond reach, he responded to the overtures of Laura Engle, a volunteer who ran the Robison poetry group. Informed of his immense portfolio of creative writing, Laura encouraged the resident to fill the emptiness of waking hours by expressing whatever emotions he was feeling in any way he thought appropriate. The rather bleak verse "Nursing Home" provides one sample:

> Here the dead are living,
> And the living ones are dead,
> In shadows lie their days to come,
> Hands cup a drooping head.
>
> Here is a pill to nurture them,
> And another one for pain,
> Another pill for sustenance,
> A painful day to gain.
>
> . . . .
> In measured pause, within the doors,
> A coweled figure waits,
> Until the laws that gave it cause,
> Signals the closing dates.

Another verse, "You Only Live Once," assumes a more ironic tone:

> You only live once
> I have heard people say.
> But once can be
> Once too often.
>
> . . . .

If I lived twice,
I would probably
Repeat the something
That made people say,
You only live once.

Once I did life twice,
And it was not so nice.
A second time
Can be as painful
As the first time.

Life and Loss

Sometime after these efforts, Laura informed Nathan of a story contest administered by the "Legacies" program of New York's Jewish Association for Services for the Aged (JASA). He responded with a semi-autobiographical sketch, "Choose Life," which described a depressed elderly widower who feels he has outlived his time. When the protagonist turns the page of a prayer book for a palsied fellow worshipper at the nursing home's Sabbath service, however, he discovers he still is of some use to another human being and garners the strength to go on.

Among six thousand nationwide entries, Nathan's sketch took fourth place. During the spring of 1993, he thrilled to the news that *HarperCollins* planned to publish an anthology of the prize-winning entries. When Laura alerted Portland's *Jewish Review*, the editors published a profile of the Robison Home's talented author.

Written expression and reading, the story explained, allowed the nursing home resident to escape the confines of his body.

"My love is writing," Nathan acknowledged.

Several days after the article ran, however, David appeared for an unexpected early morning visit. Teddy's son-in-law had called an hour earlier. Nathan's younger sister had suffered a fatal heart attack. A surviving spouse after Bernie Mass' death years earlier and a victim of painful arthritic discomfort, herself, Teddy had understood her brother's loneliness and pain. The loss was devastating, as Nathan wrote in "A Call That Will Not Come":

I listen to the telephone,
For a call that will not come.
I strain to hear a voice I've known,
But my telephone is dumb.
I scream into the plastic cone,
But the answer's dense with silence,
It has a circuit all its own,
Unknown to earthly science.

My little sister's gone away,
She'll tug my shirt no more,
The Mother Goose of yesterday,
My longing can't restore.
. . . .
My Riding Hood is gone for good,
Miss Muffett, too, and spider,
I'm seeking out Ted's neighborhood,
So I can sit besides her.

What There Was

Not long after Teddy's death, Nathan began compiling between one and two pages of meticulously typed daily entries in a personal journal.

"It is time for reflection," the very first sentence proclaimed.

His favorite colors once were earth tones, tan, brown, and gray, he began. He now preferred blue, black, and green.

His hair, once curly black and iron gray, now was white, a "suitable coloration for the tell-tale furrows" of his visage.

"The face in the mirror cannot be mine; it is an old man staring back at me," Nathan mused. Yet he added that "we better get to know each other; it is an image I cannot chase."

The most telling changes concerned mobility.

"I walk now when I used to run," he observed.

He could lower his legs to get out of bed, Nathan explained, but not lift them, requiring assistance before retiring for the night. He was even unable to dress himself.

"It is not easy from being a self-sustaining personage to a dependent in one room in a nursing facility," he confessed.

What distinguished Nathan's notations from a mere litany of

complaints, however, was the literary eloquence and disarming wit they brought to the description of his plight.

"My senses do not seem to be friends of mine," he observed on one occasion.

"I am out of tune, the maestro has led me astray," another entry reflected:

> The world that contained my symphony has shattered some of its strings. The horn section is raucous, the instrumentalists are yawning.

"My boat is leaking," Nathan noted in another segment, "and the patching and caulking can only sustain it until it must of necessity go under."

Whatever his discomforts, the Journal's author could not resist a display of sardonic wit.

"My legs are burning," he reported at one point,

> tugging at my senses for attention. Jealousy? It is a concerto but the lesser when all the vulnerable parts stage a march. Circulation carries a big banner, arthritis in robust competition, the vessels around my heart join in the big parade.

Nathan compared his battling maladies to a baseball squad.

"If one ache subsides," he noted, "a bench warming ache warms up and goes to the pitching mound."

"It is a bad day," another entry announced:

> My miserable appendages are raising hell. The hurt is taking a loud voice, it is screaming. The bed leers, it is beckoning. I give in but how long can I stay in bed? Grit my teeth and screw the surrounding world. I seek no reputation as a hero, a fighter. Do I need admiration? When it hurts, I holler, I let them know. Pain pills! Over the horizon come the pain pills. The Lone Ranger is galloping to the rescue. Heigh-ho Silver!

"I have enough ailments to distribute to a regiment," Nathan reflected one day.

"Every movement has a stab reserved for itself."

At the same time, the author observed that complaining served little use. When morphine and Tylenol could not pierce the shield of pain, he mused at one point, even the walls and ceilings were mute.

"How I would like to be restored to the status of a whole human being!" Nathan exclaimed at one point.

If he could get the Lord's ear, the author pleaded, he would ask Him why pain was a necessary adjunct to malfunctions.

Then he recalled the fifteenth century maxim that "Man proposes" while "God disposes."

Another entry referred to the lament of an old Yiddish song: "what there was, was, and is not here."

"Howling in an uninhabited wilderness," Nathan observed, "produces nothing but mocking echoes and answering cries from the denizens of the wild."

Acknowledging that he was "a strange old man," the author noted that his barking was done "behind closed doors, and is mine alone to be shared with no one."

Attempts at empathy by others usually fell flat.

"'Make the best of it,' they advise me," Nathan mimicked:

> My bitter reaction is for these soothsayers to let me alone. The pain is mine and the smugness serves for them to put a halo around their heads.

Even the Home's efforts to regulate diet and encourage exercise were problematic:

> Their idea is to prolong my life. We are at odds—they are for prolonging, I am for terminating. I am a broken record. Of what earthly use is it to keep pain-wracked, useless bodies, salvaging that which should be discarded. It is like getting the last squeeze out of the toothpaste tube. A body in a trash can awaiting the garbage collector.

"Dieting at my age hardly makes sense," he concluded.When people described Nathan as a fighter, he objected:

> Fighter? Hell, no! I am a stitched model of a human being, a bionic man. The fight they talk about has oozed out of the suture holes that stitch me together...It seems to me that I am a fighter who

must wait for the bell to ring for another round, a continuation of the match with—? I would throw the white towel in the ring if the referees would halt the bout.

Job Revisited

Nathan's loss of independence and physical vitality paled to his mourning for Dorothy, which he described as "a moat around my psyche."

"As our married years ran its course," he explained, "I came to feel that we were one entity. I came to feel that when our days were ended we would ascend the heavens hand in hand."

Yet her cancer cells "refused to be dormant," he recalled:

> They made themselves felt. My sweetheart gave those cells a valiant battle. They laughed at the chemotherapy, thumbed their nose at the radiation, and destroyed themselves by destroying Dorothy.

His frantic efforts to retain optimism, he acknowledged, did not fool his wife, who "allowed me to voice the hope that I was expending for my sake."

In the end, the disease would score what Nathan called a "daily double," taking Dorothy's life and consigning him to a black hole in space.

"I think of punishments that have been devised for man," he speculated, "and I fail to imagine anything crueler than separation such as this."

"Storied romances," he concluded, "leave indelible emotions on the unwary."

Following a comment on the greenery produced by the "weeping" of Portland rains, Nathan wondered if tears could water the foliage of a heavy heart as well. He proposed the use of mind wipers. At the same time, he tried valiantly to maintain contact with Dorothy:

> In my waking moments at times, I speak to her. But I am tackling a line no one has been able to cross. I see her image, but that is as far as I can go ... She knows that I desperately try to join her. But I cannot find the combination to her vault.

One night, however, Dorothy came to him in a hallucination. When he begged her to take him with her, she told him to be patient—there were a long list of names before his. A subsequent entry in the Journal described the ritual that accompanied late-night hours:

> My lights go out at bedtime, sleeping pill time. I tidy up my mind, my visitors arrive with sleep, when lights are low and only I can see them. The ladies of my existence, Mom, Dotty, and Teddy. Oh yes, Mom comes quite often. She knows that she gets a warm welcome. She died twenty or so years ago our time. There is no such thing as time in her present habitation. Dotty, of course, need not wait for curfew. She is with me every waking moment as well as the darkening of day.

"How my mind keeps reverting to my personal heartaches," Nathan observed. "This self-abuse is not heroic, and so it is evident that I am not the stuff heroes are made of."

Not expecting to live long after Dorothy had passed on, Nathan entertained no illusions of an extended stay at Robison. Since he viewed death as a release from suffering and "the natural course that living must take," he found the thought of additional years appalling.

The angel of death was ignoring him, Nathan contended, passing on "to those behind me, before me, to my left, and to my right."

"I should be an easy target," he complained, "but easy targets are not always his choice."

Too cynical, perhaps, to convey a literal belief in a personal God, Nathan tried talking to the heavens, but as he put it, "a hearing aid seems to be in order."

"Do you have to be a Moses to rate a miracle?" he asked at one point.

"I have developed a strange psyche," Nathan wrote on another occasion:

> I regard my afflictions as temporary nuisances on the road to total demise. I regard obituaries as a normal course, which it is, and learn the many paths that lead to extinction. Many of these are in my domain and lead me to conjecture which will be the final blow.

"I shut my eyes and stopped my breathing," the Journal confided in one passage:

It does not work. The breath forces itself back into your being and your eyes pop open, no matter what your aim is. Are our lives foreordained? Am I captain of my destiny? I think of a puppy on a leash; am I a puppy? My master tugs me where he wishes me to go.

The lamentation of many of these passages seemed reminiscent of the Book of Job. At times, ruminations about death led to questions about life's meaning.

"All through my embattlement with the evolutions of time," Nathan recalled, "I was a good boy, dutiful to home, respectful, and religious ... I never questioned the edicts that Rabbi, Hebrew School, and synagogue projected ... up to maturity this was undisputed fact."

Yet he now thought of the liturgy to the *Yizkor* memorial service that probed the Deity's relationship to Man with the query, why 'Thou Art mindful of him?'

"I will take my stricken being to the prayer bench and fight my doubts and piercing questions to my God," he confided.

Nevertheless, if he could speak "man to God," he would say the following:

> I'm absolutely no value to you here. You have already taken so many souls from my circle, why do you stop at me? I have existed beyond your three score and ten, and then some. My space in your heaven will be infinitesimal.

"I realize that my book is closing," Nathan observed on still another occasion, "but being a paperback instead of a hardcover, there will be no thud, just a soft rustling, accompanied maybe with a sigh."

"The space that my presence occupies," he noted, "will be enveloped in the mists of time."

Rather than disturbing thoughts or complaints, these were philosophical musings.

"All things come to an end," admonished the author: clothes wore out, loved ones died, and even typewriter ribbons did not have an afterlife.

His eyes were going, he wrote, and his ears were holding their hands.

"Then when all my members gang up," Nathan speculated, "they will harness me and I will go with them ... to forever after."

"I came into this world yowling," he reflected,

and I exit yowling ... but silently. To some ... it is a world of tears; to others a world of fears. With all the difficulties that dot the landscape I sometimes wonder if this world was designed for human habitation. If the answer is in the negative, we should be happy to desert it.

10

LEGACIES

ROBISON YIDDESHEH HAIM

Oh, give them a home, a *haimisheh* home,
Where the old folk in comfort can stay,
Where always is heard, an encouraging word,
And the skies are not cloudy all day.

Home, home, where it's safe,
Where bingo and blackjack are played,
Where never is heard a blasphemous word,
But the word of the Lord is obeyed.

Where *milkhik* with *flaishik* we all know is *traif*,
Cause Kosher's the name of the game.
Where never is heard a disparaging word,
In the Robison *Yiddesheh haim*.

Home, home, where it's safe,
And stresses far less, is the aim,
Where the candlelight's flare,
Lights the Friday night's prayer,
In the Robeson *Yiddesheh haim ... sweet hiam!*
In the Robison *Yiddisheh haim! ... UHMAIN!*

Nathan Horowitz
Robison Jewish Home Annual Meeting
June 8, 1994

What Else

The redeeming quality of Nathan's fatalism and despair was his desire to communicate. Words were "the garment of diverse nations, the dress of other cultures, accents of other climates ... great gifts to man," he explained in one Journal entry.

They were "like clay to be molded from the images the brain thrusts forth."

The evocation of phrases left little time for boredom. Besides, losing himself in writing allowed the Robison resident to escape morbidity.

Creativity, he insisted, "did what no pill could do for me, alleviation from pain."

To lose himself "in self-created visions," Nathan wrote, provided "a transport from the padlock that I found myself in."

The clicking typewriter had a cadence that was good for the soul, he explained.

"Page," the author wrote in one Journal passage, "you are a good companion. No back talk, docile even to erasures, even when I crumple you and consign you to the waste basket there is no remonstrance."

Retreating to his room allowed Nathan to pursue correspondence, to bury his head in books, and to devour his "scribblings," which he described as "pictures on the wall of my heart." He had not figured out where the Journal must end, he confessed, and realized his faithfulness to compiling it was hard to fathom.

"I am quite sure that no other eyes but mine will take the time to read any of it," he speculated. Yet responding to Laura Engle's prodding, he continued writing.

"There is gold in the human make-up," Nathan observed in a token of Laura's friendship, "that like a miner you must dig for it to bring it to the surface."

One Journal passage reported that Laura's husband Todd, a Robison staffer, had passed on his wife's belief that Dorothy had sent her to Nathan. At Laura's suggestion, Nathan submitted excerpts from "The Party," a sardonic poem from Mission Viejo days about a senior cocktail reception, to a contest run by the Oregon Association of Homes for the Aged:

Chattin' and noshin',
Jokin' and joshin'
It's gay here tonight,
As the punch bowl is sloshin'
The music subdued,
Is perfectly cued,
The cello and harp,
Mellow the mood.

Chuckles and laughter,
The past and hereafter,
Nostalgia and kidding,
The stories grow dafter.

It's nice here tonight,
Everything's right,
The marks of the years,
Are dimmed by soft light.

Becky and Jerry,
Are keeping things merry,
"Toast us," they laugh,
"This is no cemetery!"

Once the poem garnered certification as a Judge's Choice Winner in September 1993, Nathan received an invitation to attend the organization's First Annual Creative Writing and Poetry Festival. Making the 110-mile journey to Eugene, Oregon's Performing Arts Center, he met with the reader assigned to present the piece and felt pleased that the poem would receive suitable treatment. Festival organizers then presented each participant with a collection of award winning selections.

Two months later, *HarperCollins* released the JASA anthology under the title *Legacies: Stories of Courage, Humor, and Resilience, of Love, Loss, and Life-Changing Encounters, by New Writers Sixty and Older* (1993). Surveying its contents, Nathan pictured the collection as "an heirloom, a linkage with the past." By coincidence, Legacies appeared as a required text that term in the Portland Community College writing class attended by Gloria's daughter Kim.

To follow up the publication, Laura and David arranged for Portland's Broadway Books to host Nathan's reading of "Choose Life." Relishing the attention of an audience of thirty crowded into the store's tiny performance space, the author prompted the crowd for additional questions long after the recitation ended. The following month, Laura prevailed upon the *Jewish Review* to publish an excerpt from *The Autobiography of Nady Horowitz.* Then she placed the segment in "I Remember When," a Robison Home brochure that included Horowitz family photographs and "Pictures," a poem Nathan prepared for the occasion:

> Pictures are the fixtures in my heart.
> Each likeness has a story to impart.
> From pudgy babe to parenthood,
> Piggy-backing with my brood,
> To marching time my youth succumbs,
> To the beat of aging drums.
> The family tree is there to see,
> With the lad that once was me.
> Every part that's in my chart,
> Is in the album of my heart.

Just after the *Jewish Review* feature appeared, David and Gloria once again packed Nathan into the Chrysler for a trip to a "Doing It Their Way" caregivers' workshop at the Benedictine Institution for Long Term Care in the Oregon Willamette Valley community of Mt. Angel. Todd Engle had asked the Robison resident to compose an essay on "Autonomy," which Nathan presented at the conference.

"I seek to be an individual, addressed as such and in command of my own resources," he declared.

Respect for autonomy, observed Nathan, amounted to accepting an elderly person as a human being without allowances for age or affronts to personal dignity. To illustrate the point, Nathan singled out well-meaning people who thought nothing of peering over his shoulder to see what he was doing as he typed in the privacy of his room. In any case, he explained, dependency and depression presented lethal threats to mental health.

"Giving up the ship is waiting for the wave to drown you," Nathan warned.

Robison administrators made the presentation required reading for all staffers. Meanwhile, David's chapter of Portland's New Jewish Agenda published portions of the piece in its monthly newsletter and the *Jewish Review* ran another profile in its April edition.

"If I didn't have writing to do, I don't know what I would do," the interviewee explained.

"What else is there?"

Give Pause

Facing a host of physical and psychological obstacles, Nathan vowed to keep accepting challenges as long as he could. The opportunity to do so surfaced in June when the Home's director asked him to present a brief talk to the annual meeting of Robison officers and supporters. Beyond the friendship of Todd and Laura Engle, Nathan's Journal often took note of the kindness and thoughtfulness of a number of aides, head nurses, and managers. Yet living among the aged and often infirm, even in a well-run facility, could test the strongest of spirits, as Nathan's "Nursing Home" poem illustrated.

The Journal aptly contained several pointed descriptions of other residents.

"They float with the tide, come what may," one entry recorded:

> "Ambitions are laid to rest and they are not concerned any longer with the impressions they may project," he wrote. "Their comfort is of prime importance."

Perhaps the desire to please accounted for the surprisingly affirmative tone of Nathan's presentation. Backed by Todd on guitar and talking himself out of fear of self-humiliation before two hundred guests, he sang the lyrics of a new parody, "Robison *Yiddisheh Haim*," to the tune of "Home on the Range":

> Oh, give them a home, a *haimisheh* [home-like] home,
> Where the old folk in comfort can stay,
> Where always is heard, an encouraging word,
> And the skies are not cloudy all day.
> Home, home, where it's safe,
> Where bingo and blackjack are played,

Where never is heard a blasphemous word,
But the word of the Lord is obeyed.
Where *milkhik* [dairy] with *flaishik* [meat] we all know is *traif*
[un-kosher]
Cause Kosher's the name of the game.
Where never is heard a disparaging word,
In the Robison *Yiddesheh haim.*

Home, home, where it's safe,
And stresses far less, is the aim,
Where the candlelight's flare,
Lights the Friday night's prayer.
In the Robison *Yiddesheh haim ... sweet haim!*
In the Robison *Yiddisheh haim! ... UHMAIN!* [Amen!]

As the performance concluded, the audience rose as one in a standing ovation.

Several days later, JASA announced that Nathan had garnered another fourth place finish in the second round of the organization's senior writing contest. His entry recycled the memoir's account of the initial Lake Huntington encounter with Dorothy and her fight with cancer.

"My old age has brought some recognition," Nathan had acknowledged weeks earlier, although his sense of irony led him to characterize the belated honor as "a lop-sided swap." In truth, appreciation for his creative efforts was an issue that continued to haunt him.

"Everyone has a bug that cries to be recognized as a writer," Nathan suggested in one Journal entry. At the same time, he recalled *Tin Waltz*'s message that "a small talent at times is a minor curse rather than an attribute."

A poem from Mission Viejo days addressed these issues directly:

Give pause – and say
As you read my writ,
I comprehend
Some bit of it.

I comprehend
The reaching hand –
The proffered smile
I understand.

. . . . .

Perhaps a line,
May, too, evoke,
A mem'ry of a toast, a joke.
If you seek a smile,
And find a tear,
Flip the page
To another year.

. . . . . .

A line may cause
Your brow to knit,
Ponder not/The wit of it.
Things at time
Are best as is,
Perhaps this thought
Was only his.

Tribute

A verse written at the Robison Home re-examined the need for recognition:

Pay me tribute now,
Now, now, while my ears can hear,
And my eyes can see.

Pour me a cascade of words,
Ere the blanket of sod,
Encases and erases,
All that was me.

. . . .

Breathes there no man
With soul so dead,
That bears no pearl
Within his breast.

Smother the sardonic chuckle
With soft chiding.
A phrase, a telling word.
Your padded paw will leave the mark.

Now, now, a tribute now.
Ere the rains feed
My bouquets of tributes,
Which I will not see or hear.

Clearly, Nathan could not resist wondering about the response to his writing once he was gone.

"Revelation creeps in whether you so intended or not," he mused in one Journal entry.

"It may evoke a witty chuckle or bring a light of understanding that wa not fathomed in my breathing days."

"I suppose that in the hazy future," he speculated, "someone may pick up pieces of my 'genius' and mutter, 'Pretty good, not bad.'"

For some time, Robison's resident writer had been pressing the Home to publish his autobiography as a fundraiser but the Board thought a story about a Portland personality would be more appropriate. As an alternative, Nathan came up with the idea of an anthology of his lifelong poetry. A public reading of several pieces by Todd, Laura, and others, he suggested, could serve as a launching pad for sales to benefit the Home.

When Robison bookkeeper Nancy Golden responded to the proposal during the summer of 1994, Laura and Nathan began selecting poems for the project. Nancy then arranged for the granddaughter of the Home president to prepare a digital version of the manuscript. Nathan reported that he served as "the taskmaster, pushing and pushing, to get things rolling."

He worried that "every time a date is set for some future function I wonder if I will still be here to meet it."

Finally, Nancy delivered the prototype of the collection a few days after September 11th, Nathan's eighty-sixth birthday.

Poems Old and New: A Lifespan Collection of Verse includes an introduction by Laura Engle that pictures the volume as a documentation of a generation's inner life. Laura repeated Nathan's description of each poem as a photograph and snapshot of a particular time or place. Leading with "How Beautiful to Be a Jew," the anthology's 157 selections touched on humor, love, faith, and pride. Yet Laura pointed out that the collection's frequently dark depictions of disappointment and loss conveyed emotions rarely placed in writing by nursing home residents.

The work constituted the "records of a life honestly lived," she concluded.

Candlelight

Nathan's anthology offered an enormous sense of validation to a writer who had sought recognition through most of his life. Yet despite his concerted will and courage in the face of physical adversity, his body had declared war on his spirit. At the urging of the Home physician, the patient had consulted a vascular specialist in April only to learn he had exhausted all pharmaceutical remedies.

"Damn! Damn! Damn!" a Journal entry of the time exclaimed.

"What a rotten ending! What a miserable closing! ... My physical culture has become my physical torture."

A few days later, Nathan ruminated on "Choose Life."

"What was my mind when these words came into being?" he asked.

"Can one choose life," he persisted, "when the ultimate is death when one chooses it or not? Pain pays no attention to whatever one chooses."

"The poetry that I am now writing," Nathan confessed in June, "emerges with a black band around my arm. It is morbid." A new work, he reported, "came out with a sardonic twist."

At one point, Nathan acknowledged he no longer could control his moods.

"They ask no questions," he observed, "they simply sweep in and take charge. I am simple prey for these marauders."

As the Jewish New Year approached in September 1994, the Journal unleashed a wave of fury:

> How happy can a new year be when the dancing is a wheel chair polka? A new year is a projection into the future. How futile this idea is when the future is a wish for extinction. This is not a despondent line of prayer, rather I class it as a longing, a cessation of the disagreeable crisis that is linked together into one chain of existence.

"Perhaps these notes that I am putting forth will find tinges of contempt with you," he addressed the reader.

"But the truth of the matter is that I am past caring."

Several days later, the very last Journal entry anticipated Nancy Golden's delivery of the anthology manuscript. Merely a week after that, Nathan suffered another fall, requiring several days in the hospital.

"Nat, it's up to you," a sympathetic attending physician instructed.

"You've got to decide if you want to go on with this or not. There's not much for us to do either way."

He never did answer. Still, he agreed to return to Robison, where the normally crotchety resident admitted it was nice to be home again. Through the early autumn, Nathan conducted several meetings to plan a publication party for the anthology. Drawing on his experience in sales, he sought to maximize distribution.

"The writer is a cook, and the cooking he or she produces must be palatable or the diner goes elsewhere," he once explained in a Journal entry.

An advocate of "down-to-earth simplicity," Nathan insisted that authors should not strive for language unfamiliar to their tongue.

"Write clearly and do not drown your product with unwieldy words," he had suggested in another segment, an approach he compared to a painter who seeks a simple delineation.

He cautioned that it was important to leave the impression that the content of the anthology would "not be esoteric alone," but "appeal to the more popular demand of simple understanding."

Despite Nathan's sense of urgency, arrangements for getting the book into production still were not in place by mid-October. Frustration over his failing body, moreover, fueled increased irritability toward nurses and aides. At a special session to air his grievances, Nathan got angry when David appeared to side with Robison employees. Privately, his son tried to make the point that his father was dependent on the staff's goodwill and needed to get along out of pure self-interest.

Things remained at this impasse as the pains intensified over the next two weeks, leading to increased morphine dosages and further deterioration. One night Nathan tried to phone the desk only to inadvertently dial 911 and bring out the rescue squad. By the last week of October, he was bedridden, no longer eating, and gradually shutting down.

At that point, the head nurse took David aside. That afternoon, he selected a casket at a local funeral home, completed arrangements to send the remains to Newport Beach, and summoned Michael from California.

For the next two days, Michael, Gloria, and David maintained a bedside vigil. Seeking to ensure Nathan's comfort at one point, David applied a wet rag to his father's dry mouth, a gesture the patient interpreted as an effort to force him to take nourishment.

"What do you think is going on here?" Nathan shot back with annoyance.

That was the last thing he ever said to his son or anyone else.

Later that evening, the Robison office called. When David and Gloria returned, they found a nurse sitting by Nathan's bed reading his poetry by candlelight.

11

ECHOES

NATHAN HOROWITZ
(1908-1994)

POEMS OLD & NEW
A LIFE SPAN COLLECTION

Sunday, November 27th
1:30 p.m.

PLEASE JOIN US IN A LOVING MEMORIAL READING
OF NATHAN HOROWITZ'S AGELESS POEMS

READING BY FRIENDS & FAMILY

ROBISON JEWISH HOME
6125 SW BOUNDARY ST.
PORTLAND, OR 97221

THE BOOK IS DISTRIBUTED BY THE ROBISON JEWISH HOME

copies will be sold at the event

Two on the Aisle

Repeating the treatment afforded Dorothy, the Robison Home followed the Jewish ritual of spiritual purification by arranging for the overnight washing of Nathan's body. Two days after an impromptu service at the Home, David, Michael, and Gloria flew to Newport Beach.

David recited two of Nathan's poems at the gravesite. The first was "Final Sleep":

> The last buttock of my fence jumping sheep,
> Has achieved at last my final sleep.
> No more need I alleviate
> The faithful pains of vertebrate.
>
> No more will I have to cup an ear
> To hear voices as from stratosphere,
> Nor demand a stronger light
> To compensate my struggling sight.
>
> To tie a lace, to reach, to stand,
> I'm grateful, no more helping hand.
> And images of dear friends gone,
> My tortured head won't dwell upon.
>
> So all in all, in restful sleep,
> Why, dear hearts, do you weep?

Then he read "Two on the Aisle":

> The strata and the echelon,
> That my life revolves upon,
> Though not completely woebegone,
> Is a flight or two beyond the john.
>
> My influence can tip no scale,
> My fragile weight wouldn't move a snail,
> To seek a favor strikes me dumb,
> A battered loaf leaves me a crumb.

Procuring seats upon a dais,
The very best that I can say is,
My face gets flushed with battle won,
If I'm enthroned on balc'ny one!

. . . .

With grit and wit and firm intent,
I faced my Temple's president,
To implement my last advent.
– The wifely prod is evident –

I insisted like the man I am
To scan the graveyard diagram,
I proudly stated I couldn't be moved,
Until my dictate was approved!

I scarcely could contain my smile,
At last I got me two on the aisle!

Days later, David and Michael agreed to absorb the printing costs of Nathan's anthology so the Robison Home could benefit from the proceeds. The long-awaited reading and book sale took place before some hundred guests in the Robison common room in late November. The printed program, assembled by Todd and Laura, included family photographs, the list of selected poems and readers, and a biographical portrait. Following the recitations, Michael delivered a hearty vocal of "Chicken Dinnah!" with David at the piano, a replay of Roslyn Heights days.

The lyrics' signature couplet appeared in the program at the close of Nathan's biography:

Thank the Lord for the good things!
There's nothin' better than the good things!

Markers

Weeks after the reading, David and Michael delivered a $5,000 donation to the Oregon Cultural Heritage Commission to help fund a local poetry park. The project centered on Hazel Hall, a nationally acclaimed Northwest Portland poet of the 1920s who had produced her work while confined to a wheelchair. Nathan had attended a reading of *Monograms*, a new play about the writer by dramatist Sue Mach. With additional grants in hand, the OCHC commissioned graphic artist John Laursen to install three granite tablets inscribed with samples of Hall's poetry as well as an illustrated biographical plaque. At the dedication at the site on Mother's Day, 1995, David explained that he and Michael saw the undertaking as a chance to honor their parents' devotion to poetry, prose, and drama—essential ingredients of any vital culture.

In July, Gloria and David drove to southern California to meet Michael for the unveiling of Nathan's tombstone, a trip that included a game at Dodger Stadium in a gesture to baseball's place in family lore. To match the dedication on Dorothy's memorial, the words "FATHER HUSBAND LYRICIST" appeared on Nathan's tablet.

Three months later, in October 1995, David and Gloria took possession of a second home in the Oregon North Coast community of Arch Cape. The inspiration for the project dated back to a Christmas break in Mission Viejo when David had distracted himself from the deterioration of Dorothy's health by sitting at the kitchen table and designing a fantasy beach getaway. In a casual outing to the Coast several months later, he and Gloria came across a vacant acre of hillside forestland a quarter-mile east up the hill from the beach.

"You could own this!" Gloria exclaimed.

David eventually pursued the idea. Once Nathan eased the way by providing both sons a $5,000 gift from the family trust, David dipped into personal savings to complete the purchase of what Gloria called "the last bargain on the Coast." Anxious about untrustworthy contractors and the headaches of taking on a major project, Nathan pleaded with his son to postpone construction plans until he was gone. Accordingly, it was not until early 1995 that David and Gloria approached a local builder.

When completed, the Arch Cape getaway sat at the top of the sloping property, where it afforded a distant glimpse of the ocean beyond a spread of full-grown spruce, hemlock, and cedar. Adhering to David's original design, the two-bedroom, one-and-a-half bath, 1,200-square foot house emulated the rustic appeal that Nathan loved with natural board-and-batten cedar siding, a red metal roof, and wood-framed windows. In a nod to Catskill bungalows, the interior walls and ceiling featured knotty tongue-and-groove paneling with wide larch boards for the country-style flooring. Yellow Formica countertops in the kitchen, utility room, and bathroom, a throwback to 1950s décor, sustained the motif.

David's design called for open space between the living room, kitchen, and dining area with a half-wall divider providing a buffer between his childhood upright piano and the kitchen workspace. A corner wood stove with a river rock setting served as the focal point of the living room. On the opposite end, a bevy of windows opened the dining alcove to a southwest exposure and a wraparound deck. In the master bedroom, wall-to-wall windows looked out to the forest.   By the time the beach house was ready, Nathan and Dorothy's "sleepy hollow" reclining chair, cobbler's bench coffee table, fruitwood TV cabinet, and quirky Early American lamp had found their way to the Portland house. The storage bin now supplied Arch Cape with David's childhood desk, Nathan's stereo tuner, two upholstered chairs, several wall hangings, and the oak bedroom dressers from 1938. At Gloria's suggestion, a coastal woodcrafter incorporated the carved headboards of the matching twin bed set into two cedar blanket chests.

In June 1996, eight months after spending their first weekend at the coastal retreat, David and Gloria consummated their ten-year relationship with an outdoor wedding on the deck. However much Nathan liked and admired Gloria, David had been reluctant to reintroduce the sensitive prospect of intermarriage. Former Portland judge and onetime mayor of nearby Cannon Beach Herb Schwab now performed the honors before 175 guests. Beyond the Hebrew blessing for wine and traditional exchange of vows, the ceremony included recitations from the Old Testament and a diversity of literary texts and presentations by Michael; Gloria's son, daughter, and sister; and several friends. A catered buffet of grilled salmon and vegetable salad followed.

By request, poet Tim Barnes, who served as master of ceremonies, invoked the memory of Gloria's father and Nathan and Dorothy while noting that neither Gloria's mother nor an increasingly frail Mickey Levine could make the trip. Mickey had rebounded from his stroke eight years earlier and served two terms as president of the Friends of the North Miami Beach Library, a position he used to lobby for increased state funding for public agencies. He would take great pride in helping Bill Clinton carry Florida and return to the White House for a second term in 1996. Despite all his disappointments, he had never given up the dream of a better world.

"Even if doomed to failure," Mickey urged in one letter, "we must keep up the fight or there is no purpose in living."

Although Mickey was now eighty-two, it came as a shock to learn that on November 22nd, the anniversary of John Kennedy's assassination, he had suffered a fatal home accident. The culprit was a sweet roll warming up in the toaster for an afternoon snack. When the spring on the old appliance stuck, a fire engulfed the apartment with deadly smoke. Emergency medics found Mickey unconscious on the front hallway floor and were not able to revive him.

David's first thought was that he had let Dorothy down by not looking out for her brother as she requested that last week in Mission Viejo. Yet there was no need to fly to Florida since Mickey's instructions ruled out a funeral and called for the dispersal of his ashes at sea. As an act of commemoration nonetheless, David hired a graduate student several months later to transcribe the handwritten reminiscence his uncle had produced years earlier.

What Made Mickey Run? Episodes from the Memoirs of Milton David Levine (1999) emerged from the effort. Photocopied from the digital manuscript, the collection covered the author's recollections of childhood and his political activities up through the 1980s. Besides David's brief biography and the *New York Times* obituary prepared by former AVC and ADA cohorts, the volume included the *Times* article on Mickey's resignation from ADA in 1975 and a *Newsweek* photo of his submitting to arrest during the anti-draft protests of 1980.

A tribute from Michael focused on his uncle's ability to run a meeting with an absolute mastery of Robert's Rules of Order. David celebrated the Trotskyist who wore fine suits, smoked expensive cigars, hailed New York cabs in abandon, lunched at exquisite midtown cafés, loved opera and theater, and preferred rye on the rocks. Most of all, he remembered his uncle's devotion to social justice. Appropriately, proceeds from the sale of the collection went to several of Mickey's favorite causes, including the North Miami Beach Public Library, the United Farm Workers, and Americans for Peace Now.

Reverberations

Unlike Mickey, Nathan and Dorothy regretted not having more influence on Michael and David. The couple quietly lamented that their sons were not fervent Zionists. Yet a shared political pragmatism and understanding of *realpolitik* pushed both generations toward areas of agreement. For

David, the need to adjust expectations over his mother's failing health had reinforced a sense that not all problems had optimal solutions. This anti-utopian posture surfaced when Iraq's Saddam Hussein engineered an invasion of neighboring Kuwait in 1990 three weeks before Dorothy's death. Accepting U.S. involvement in the Gulf War as a legitimate response to territorial aggression, David found himself questioning the peace movement's opposition to all use of force. As Iraq reacted to a U.S. bombing campaign with haphazardly directed missile strikes on Israeli targets, moreover, he took to the campus newspaper to condemn West Bank Palestinians for cheering on a ruthless dictator who had no real interest in their cause.

When Yasir Arafat, Israeli Prime Minister Yitzhak Rabin, and President Bill Clinton gathered at the White House in September 1993 to commit to a peace settlement within five years, David welcomed the gesture as a vindication of activists who refused to demonize Israel and held both sides accountable for the compromises essential for a deal. Not surprisingly, Nathan did not share such optimism. Although he was willing to concede the theoretical *desirability* of an agreement, nothing could convince him of its *likelihood*.

"God Bless You," he exclaimed following the ceremony, "but I tell you, Davey, I won't live to see it—there'll never be peace between the Arabs and the Jews."

Even so, an entry in Nathan's Journal acknowledged that pessimism over a possible accord "should not cloud the staunching of blood."

For his part, Michael would make a point of visiting Israel on a world tour at the turn of the year 2000 although both sons subsequently had to admit that their father's pessimism over Middle East peace prospects seemed borne out by events.

With David twice divorced and Michael single, a thornier issue involved the question of grandchildren and the perpetuation of Jewish heritage. Nathan's Journal recalled David's comment that the prospect was "not in the cards."

"The name 'Horowitz' is grinding down to extinction," a saddened father observed—"unwept, un-honored, and unsung." "There is no offspring from either David or Mike," he lamented. "Delving into the future is a blind alley for me," Nathan confessed.

"I have produced sons—the sons should be cognizant of what is to be."

David A. Horowitz

Carrying On

Undoubtedly, the prospective termination of the family line haunted Nathan and Dorothy Horowitz. Yet as role models who bridged material, artistic, and spiritual endeavors; as advocates of ethical standards of social justice; as admirers of learning and critical thought; as dedicated artisans of the written text; and as instinctive and ironic humorists and dramatists; they passed on a rich and multifaceted legacy with distinct Jewish shadings.

One can see a passion for the life of the mind and a wit-infused interplay of physical and metaphysical realms in both *A Freak's Anthology* and *Equator*, Michael's early works. He struck a similar tone in *Sunbelt Stories* (1994, a compendium of three tales that defied arbitrary distinctions between reality and the supernatural. Echoing Dorothy's aversion to violence and Nathan's respect for the natural world, the book's final segment features a pod of Pacific humpback whales who plead for reconciliation with the humans who once hunted them down.

Michael's next project, *Split Creek: War Novel of the Deep West* (2006), took on the clash of twentieth century political ideals that intersected his parents' lives. The story follows a young man in Nazi Germany who witnesses his Communist mother's arrest by the Gestapo. After he joins Hitler Youth to hide his background and serves in German Army intelligence, he winds up in a U.S. prisoner-of-war camp in Wyoming. A ruinous liaison with the mystic daughter of a Nazi sympathizer ultimately leads to his appreciation of American democratic liberalism. As the book ends, the former soldier appears as an elderly political science professor who has fused his mother's socialist political ideals with the Judeo-Christian values of his adopted homeland.

"Finally, I'm my mother's son," the protagonist declares in the very last line.

Michael's *Downmind*, a novella released by a New Zealand science fiction publisher in 2013, echoed the interests of both parents in a somber psychological and environmental fantasy with unsettling reverberations of the Holocaust. Michael even mirrored Nathan's lifetime fascination with Hollywood by converting the work into a screenplay prototype.

The ties between metaphysical and physical spheres, long a subject of Michael's journalism, define much of his scholarly work as well. In 1996, the *Journal of Indo-European Studies* published his essay on the fusion of pagan and scientific worldviews in Ancient Greece. The journal subsequently printed his article on the vitality of Iceland's traditional communal society. To fulfill the terms of a Peace Corps assignment to the South Pacific island kingdom of Tonga in the late-Nineties, Michael worked as a tourism development adviser and taught Sociology at the 'Atenisi Institute, a small liberal arts academy. Returning to Tonga in 2007, he served as dean and instructor in the Institute's social science and humanities program. He followed this with a series of summer visiting scholar appointments in Hawaii, Australia, and New Zealand involving presentations on Greek science, German philosophy, Tongan democratic politics, South Pacific youth, and the craft of screenwriting.

Like Michael, David has carried on his parents' passion for writing. Beyond textbook revisions and a variety of periodical articles, he has produced four U.S. history books and a memoir in the years since Nathan's death. Each addresses the interplay of social justice and populism that Nathan and Dorothy embodied. *Beyond Left and Right: Insurgency and the Establishment* (1997) outlines a political tradition opposing big money, unwieldy government, and ideological pretension. *Inside the Klavern: The Secret History of a 1920s Ku Klux Klan* (1999) traces the reassertion of traditional social values to the impact of wrenching moral change. *America's Political Class under Fire: The Twentieth Century's Great Culture War* (2003), focuses on critics of elite modernist and cosmopolitan mores. *The People's Voice: A Populist Cultural History of Modern America* (2008) aims for an accessible approach by tying samples of expressive popular culture to the experience and aspirations of ordinary people.

The populist sensibilities of David's scholarship have found a parallel in his teaching methods. Tapping a family-rooted flair for dramatization and humor in informal lectures, David has shied away from fashionable curriculum innovations in favor of disciplined essays from his students. His impatience with pedagogic pretensions and imperial administrators owed much to the standards of fair play, integrity, and thoughtful realism he attributed to his parents' example.

For years, David recognized the West commissions that had financed the bulk of his education by carrying his lecture notes in Nat Harris' leather sample bag. He traced his penchant for organizing and promoting academic forums and community cultural events to Nathan's sales and theatrical talents as well as Dorothy's organizational know how and commitment to learning. For a tribute to the Oregon work of 1930s documentary photographer Dorothea Lange, for example, David followed his parents' example by creating a dramatic script from the artist's on-site notations that four readers recited during PowerPoint demonstrations of the images.

Whatever misgivings and disappointments Nathan and Dorothy shared, their life offers a remarkable story. The tale begins as a Depression romance between two unlikely offspring of working-class immigrants, one from a family of secular Jewish socialists, the other from an Orthodox upbringing, who nearly go their separate ways. The two then transcend the differences in their backgrounds and marginal levels of material security to fashion a close-knit family in the years after World War II. The success each ultimately finds in their chosen profession, together with their exodus from the West Bronx to suburban Long Island and then to California, offers a tantalizing glimpse of the American and Jewish experience of middle-class social mobility and assimilation.

What sets the couple apart, however, is their insistent search for distinction.

Despite the frustrations and reverses each experiences, neither ever loses sight of the liberating forces of intellect, creativity, humor, and self-reflection that make existence more than a test of survival. With little prospect of reward or recognition, each marks the span of their lives with written testaments to their hopes, fantasies, and regrets. Not all efforts were of equal import. Neither of the two exerted a monumental influence on the world. Nor were they immune to the demons, insecurities, or conventional pieties that intersect most lives. Yet their insistence on asserting themselves as individuals willing to reach beyond the expectations of others, and the candor, occasional grace, playfulness, and moments of wisdom that culminate in their ultimate confrontation with mortality, certainly rank as the highest of achievements.

The storied romance of Nathan and Dorothy Horowitz, the son and daughter of struggling immigrants, offers its share of insights into the arduous path to middle-class respectability and the complex and contradictory strands of the twentieth century Judaic American experience. It was their mutual love affair with the written word, however, that enabled them to address sensibilities that both incorporated and transcended the experience of generational cohorts. This creative vitality, and the honesty, courage, and humility each brought to their modest successes and assorted challenges, remains their most enduring legacy.

David A. Horowitz

APPENDIX

With our young and with our old we will go
Exodus 10:9

On her eightieth birthday, her quavering voice said to me,
"You didn't have to do this, this thing that you have done.
I am old and the warmth of your love
Is gift enough for me my son."

I wrapped the coat around her frail old form,
I kissed the wrinkles around her brimming eyes,
"Your new coat is only lovely now," I said,
"Reflecting the soul that with it lies."

In quavering tones the old Torah spoke, its parchment
   cracked and patched,
"You didn't have to do this, this thing that you have done,
I am old and the warmth of your love
Is gift enough for me, my son."

I beheld the ark – Magnificent! Vibrant! New!
Yet I wet the old with my brimming eyes,
"Only because of thee," I said, "this shrine will shine,
Reflecting the light that within it lies."

And thus it shall be, as we have always told,
We will go with our young and with our old.

Nathan Horowitz

GENESIS RE-TOLD

And it came to pass that the earth was full of fallout
From the multitude of nations,
And the Lord looked upon his green fields
And felt a heaviness in heart,
For, lo, they would be green no more.

And he looked upon the men who had multiplied themselves
And he felt a great anger.
For they were about to destroy His Earth, yea,
The very Earth He had flooded in the days of Noah.

For what hath Man learned?
To kill and be killed!

And the Lord cried out in great anger,
"I AM DONE WITH THEE!"
And behold, even I shall bring forth destruction
   hotter than the sun, deadlier than death,
   that no green thing, no creeping thing

Shall survive My anger:
For ye who must have need of war
When there is peace,
For ye who must seek death
Where there is life,
For ye who must play falsely
When there is truth,
For ye who dwell in ugliness
When there is beauty.

My heart is full of bitterness –
I AM DONE WITH ALL OF THEE!

And a youth looked up at the Lord,
And as he clasped his wife's small hand,
He whispered shyly up to him,
"Have mercy, Lord, for we two are young
And have not learned full courage
And we are sore afraid."

And the Lord remembered his covenant of the Flood,
And the youth and his gentle wife found grace in His eyes.
Behold, I am the Lord, and I say unto thee,
Build thyself a ship to fly
Through all the spaces of the stars,
And take upon yourself the right
To choose five other youths
And their goodly wives,
So that you may be safe from destruction.
FOR THE EARTH SHALL NO LONGER BE!

And the youth did what the Lord commanded him to do.

He chose a doctor to heal the sick,
For whosoever longs to heal can never kill,
And that was of the first.

And then he chose a farmer,
For whosoever loves growing things
Cannot bear to see anything die.
And that was the second choice.

And then he chose a carpenter,
For whosoever builds
Cannot bear to destroy.
And that was the third.

And then he chose an artist,
For whosoever creates
   what has never been written
      or played
         or sung
            or molded
               or told before –
For whosoever dreams dreams for men –
Cannot bear to annihilate.
And that was of the fourth.

Then, last, he chose a teacher of books,
For whosoever seeks to instruct
   the young, the old
   the helpless, the ignorant,

Lights the flaming fires of Love and Learning,
And, thus, he cannot do violence.

And then these chosen were safely placed in their ship of space,
Sailing through the spheres,
It came to pass that a great heat fell upon the earth,
And, lo, the waters dried,
And the green shriveled,
And no creeping thing crept,
And no living thing lived,
And the Lord turned his back on the Earth
That was no longer the earth
   but .....cold.....black.....stone.

Dorothy Horowitz   November 1961

CHRONOLOGICAL LIST OF PUBLISHED WORKS

Dorothy Levine:

"Emerson in the Twentieth Century," *Perwinkle* [Walton High School, The Bronx, New York], 1933

"The College Comments on Fascism," *Echo* [Hunter College of the City of New York], January 1938

"Poem," *Echo* [Hunter College of the City of New York], January 1938

Dorothy Horowitz:

"Mrs. Blight Goes Abnormal," radio script on public housing [Political Action Committee of Congress of Industrial Organizations], 1944

"Tribute to the Substitute," *K-Six* [Board of Education of the City of New York], Fall 1961

"Counselor, What Would You Do? *The School Counselor* [American School Counselor Association], May 1969

"The Survivor, A Play," *North Coast Times Eagle*, September 1988

"A Baseball Fan Fights Cancer," *North Coast Times Eagle*, October–November 1988

"Welcome: Do Not Enter," *North Coast Times Eagle*, March 1989

"Twilight Village, *North Coast Times Eagle*, May–June 1990

Bread-and-Butter Lines, desktop publication, 1994, Horowitz Family Archives

Nathaniel Harris:

Lyricist, "Along de way to Hebbin'," Carl Fischer, Inc., 1937

Lyricist, "Don' Ask Me Lawd," G. Schirmer, Inc., 1939

Lyricist, "De Lawd's Dress Suit," G. Schirmer, Inc., 1939

Lyricist, "Chicken Dinnah!" G. Schirmer, Inc., 1941

Nat Harris:

Tin Waltz, 1954 [staged by Actors and Writers Theater, New York City, April–May 1954]

Nathan Horowitz:

"A Christmas Incident," *The Forward*, August 21, 1978

"I Remember Soho," *The Forward*, June 6, 1982

"A Visit from My Father," *The Forward*, September 12, 1982

"The Bosses Should Boin!" *The Forward*, November 14, 1982

"The Buyer Said a Merry Christmas" (1937), excerpts in *Los Angeles Times*, December 15, 1982

"Letter to a Memory," *The Forward*, January 16, 1983

"Louis Abramson Died," *The Forward*, February 11, 1983

"Geneshe," *The Forward*, February 25, 1983

"One Tongue" *The Forward*, April 29, 1983

"Twilight in Jerusalem," *The Forward*, May 27, 1983

"G-d and the World Series," *The Forward*, December 5, 1986

"Dedication of the Ark," *North Coast Times Eagle*, September 1988

"I am Worried," B'nai B'rith Record [Councils of B'nai B'rith in Southern California], January 1989

"Keep Off the Grass," *North Coast Times Eagle*, June 1989

"Four Chaplains" (1943), *North Coast Times Eagle*, January–February 1990

"Choose Life," *Legacies: Stories of Courage, Humor, and Resilience, of Love, Loss, and Life-Changing Encounters, by New Writers Sixty and Older* [Jewish Association for the Aging], 1993

"The Pier," *A Collection of Poetry Written by Residents of Oregon's Retirement and Nursing Homes* [Oregon Association of Homes for the Aging], 1994

Poems Old and New, Robison Jewish Home, 1994

Milton D. Levine:

"What Made Mickey Run? Episodes from the Memoirs of Milton D. Levine," 1999, State Historical Society of Wisconsin and American Jewish Historical Society, Brandeis University

CPSIA information can be obtained
at www.ICGtesting.com
Printed in the USA
FFHW021041112041 9
516733S8-5717FF